MW00426226

# AGILE UNEMPLOYMENT

## YOUR GUIDE TO THRIVING WHILE OUT OF WORK

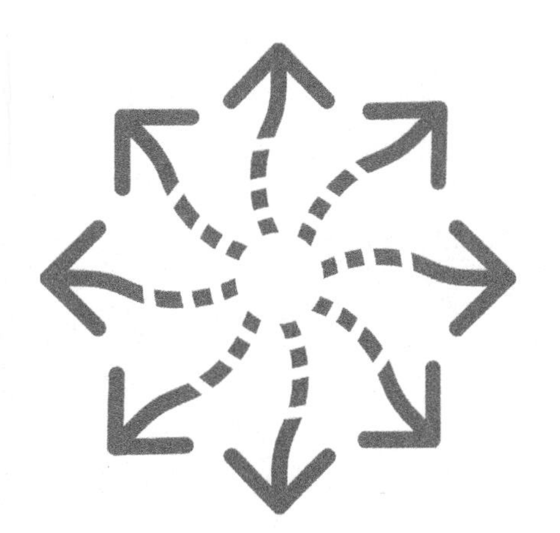

SABINA SULAT

Re: Working
Washington, DC 20002



First hardcover edition 2021 (or) Published 2021

ISBN 978-1-7377183-3-8 (hardcover)
ISBN 978-1-7377183-0-7 (paperback)
ISBN 978-1-7377183-2-1 (ePub)
ISBN 978-1-7377183-1-4 (Kindle)

# ACKNOWLEDGMENTS

This is the book you hope to never write and hope no one needs to read. However, I would be remiss if I did not thank those who were instrumental in helping me through my *re: working* journey. My hope for you, Reader, is that you have a fantastic team supporting you while you return to work just like I did while I was unemployed.

A special thank you to these people, in no particular order:

**Lara** — We sometimes try to figure out why we are friends, but in the end, we always realize that we could not do without each other. Thank you for all the love and support through good times and bad. There is not enough wine and cake in the world to thank you for all you have done for me.

**Gigi** — For the countless "workdays" and pep talks. How could we have gone through our last two years of college, shared a senior year core group, barely remember each other and yet now I cannot imagine my life without you?

**Babak** — For your quiet wisdom and unlimited support. You're a constant voice of logic and reason, often when I don't want it but always when I need it. No one else makes me look at things in a better light than you.

**Deirdre** — You came back into my life at the perfect time. We were irreversibly connected from the first moment we met. Somehow, the universe decided we had to be friends, and the universe, as always, was right.

**Gina** — You are always the leader of the world's smallest street gang. How did I get so lucky to call you a friend?

**California** — You are indeed my soulmate. I know you are supporting me, even though we never talk as often as we should.

**Stephanie, Amanda, Chris B., Phelosha, Mary, Martha, Sandy, Ian** — You are the best friends and colleagues a girl could have.

Special Thanks

**Shauna** — My friend and mentor. I aspire to be you and I always fall short, yet you always think the best of me. You have always believed in me professionally and always supported me personally. The blog and this book all happened because of your quiet but constant insistence that I could do anything I put my mind to. If only everyone had a Shauna, the world would be filled with confident achievers.

**Andy** — Where would I be if you had not reached out to me on LinkedIn? I can't even begin to imagine.

**Honorée**—It takes a gifted person to inspire those who do not know them. I am forever grateful.

# TABLE OF CONTENTS

# PREFACE

I could never have imagined the ripple effect that would come from losing my job. I had no idea it would take me almost a year to find a new one. And I didn't know that my job hunt would encounter peaks and valleys and ungodly rabbit holes. I didn't know that because of dire needs, I'd have to take a job that was two levels beneath where I had been. As I searched for work, I occasionally thought about writing a book. Who amongst us hasn't either had the thought themselves or had someone come up to them and say, "You should write a book.?"

Truth is, HR is a particularly rich field for book ideas—most Human Resource professionals have stories that are mind-blowing and equally true. My thoughts of writing a book to share my experience with others came and went. Once I found work again, I was devoted to my new job, cushioned by the feeling of safety, security, and gratefulness that came with it. As the reality of the COVID-19 pandemic began to be felt in the United States, the chaotic economy made my pipe dream of writing a luxury. Or so I thought.

Who knew a virus bringing the world to a virtual stop would be the flintstone that would reignite the sparks of my dream? It all happened suddenly and unexpectedly on a Thursday afternoon. The day before, career coach Andy Storch had reached out to my un-updated LinkedIn account and had asked to connect. My LinkedIn profile still had enough juice to bring visitors to my profile despite my year of unemployment. Andy invited me to his Hot Seat podcast and book coach, Honorée Corder, was his guest. Honorée described book writing as the route to becoming an instant expert in your field as well as boosting your street cred. While listening to the podcast, I was texting my friend, Babak, saying that I'd have been helping so many people if I had come around to writing my book on unemployment. Dear sweet Babak, ever the optimist, said that I could write it now and it would still be of value. It was as if three highly intelligent, capable, supportive people on Team Sabina were telling me that I could and should do this. As if it was my duty to myself and others. How could I say no? You just do not get that kind of support most of the time (as an aside, isn't that a problem in our world?). All of that as a result of the encouragement in conjunction with the Maryland shelter-in-place order and the gift of free time, I was able to set about my personal mission, thanks in part to the elimination of my commute. By promising to wisely use the gift of time and a commitment to write two hours or 500 words a day—whichever came first—I was able to create a book, or the start of one.

In additional to my own experience and insights from being out of work, I bring my professional skills to this book. I have spent the better part of a decade and a half in the field of Talent Management. I have studied how HR works within an organization as well as how organizations leverage their employees' skill sets to meet goals and strategy. In writing this book, I have set out to do three things. The first is to give readers a comprehensive timeline and guide to the obligations you need to complete while out of work to ensure that losing your job will have a minimal negative impact on you, your family, your finances, and your career path. Second, to increase readers' awareness of the more subtle but equally important things you might experience while out of work, such as the immediate and long-term impact that unemployment will have on your mental health and well-being. My aim is to enlighten readers on certain influences so they can recognize them and address them when they occur. It's vital for your health. Finally, I wish to share my personal returning-to-work story to let you know that you are not alone in this journey and that you are not the only one to think and feel the things you are experiencing.

To effectively use this book, I recommend flipping through the sections and concentrating on what speaks to you the most at a given time. Being out of work is a highly debilitating experience. You will go through good days and bad. This period will test your wallet and your soul. If you are in a phase where you need practical advice on how to get by, you may want to look at one of the more tactical sections of this book so you can prepare for an interview or apply for unemployment. If you are going through a period of sadness or depression, you might find comfort in the self-care sections. If you are searching for the right direction for your career path, you might want to go to the section on writing your vision and mission statements so that you can discover your passion and capitalize on your next move.

As a seasoned learning professional, I know that we can learn a lot from our mistakes. I have made plenty, enough to have teaching and leadership material for decades. Most of the time, I navigated the underbelly of unemployment on my own. As other friends lost their jobs due to the economic downturn brought on by COVID implications, I became their Unemployment Guru and I guided them through the practical and emotional aspects of unemployment. My hope is that this book will guide you on your journey.

The truth is, no book can magically provide you with a new job. However, I offer something different than magic: I want to help you get back to work and I am providing some insights to that end. One of the most frustrating things about unemployment is navigating the process alone. Not just filing for benefits or writing my resume, but all the things that no one talks about. There was the isolation. The lack of structure. The challenge to add meaning to my day-to-day life. How to tell friends and my network that I was out of work. As if that wasn't difficult enough, no one prepared me for how I would feel once I returned to working. When I landed a great, new job, I didn't feel whole.

With this book, I will prepare you for unemployment life and the emotions that come with it. My hope is that by following even portions of this book, you will minimize the impact being out of work has on your finances and your well-being. I want to help you use this time so that you can return to work stronger, more confident and more resilient.

I am a huge fan of Morten Hansen and his amazing book -- *Great at Work*. In the book, he writes that we excel at work when we combine passion and purpose. I have since discovered that (1.) HR and Talent Management is my purpose. (2.) Helping other people is my passion. After I finished writing my book, it has become clear that helping others build confidence and resilience while they are unemployed allows me to combine my passion and my purpose. While I wish no one would ever need this book, I hope that those who need it will find it helpful. All I ask in return is that they find a way to pay it forward—to share the wisdom of their journey and success with someone else to teach, to support, and to inspire them.

# THE HOLE

There is a small parable of the man who was walking down the street and suddenly fell into a great hole. The hole was dark and he couldn't see. The sides of the hole were slippery and steep, and he could not pull himself out. The hole was so deep he could barely hear the world above him.

He yelled and cried for help, but no one came. Finally, he heard footsteps above and called out for help. It was a doctor passing by. The man yelled to her that he was in a hole and needed help. She stopped and floated down a prescription to him, but it was of no help.

Again, the man waited until he heard another set of footsteps approach, and he yelled and cried for help. A clergyman was passing by and offered to pray for him. Although the prayers made him feel better, he was still in the hole.

Finally, the man heard another set of footsteps and a stranger approached. The man cried out for help. Suddenly, the stranger jumped down into the hole with the man.

The man was incredulous. "Why, why did you do this? Now we are both in the hole!" he exclaimed.

"Yes," said the stranger. "But I have been in this hole before, and I know the way out."

***Right now, you are in a hole. You might be feeling alone and wondering how you are going to get out. I, Reader, have been in this hole. Together, we will get out.***

# HOW I LOST MY DREAM JOB

When I look back, what I recall most is that I had an eerie sense of calm. None of it was a surprise to me. I cannot recall the exact moment I felt the shift—when I knew the inevitable was coming. When it happens like that, you go with it. You have no choice but to let things happen. You come in and you do your day-to-day to the best of your abilities. You work as if you have a future, even when you realize you don't. Because, what else can you do? I do recall that things started to feel different. I started to detach and maybe that is what saved me. It is almost as if I had received a diagnosis that I had a terminal disease. It makes you live your life waiting for the inevitable. You start looking for signs you are wrong, even when you know you are right.

When I started this job, I was so optimistic. When I was offered the role, I thought I had finally arrived — think Melanie Griffith at the end of *Working Girl.* Finally, it felt like my life plan was falling into place. I had been doing executive work in prior jobs, and now I finally had that coveted title at a prestigious organization. My five-year plan was pretty set: Do my best here (really, I intended to kick ass), get my Ph.D., and set the path to become an expert in organization development/learning and the workplace. As an employee, I had the opportunity to further my education and to further develop skills such as presentation, executive presence, and leadership. I approached this role with two purposes: (1.) It would allow me to earn a living at something I do best (2.) It would help me prepare for the final phase of my career. I knew it would take time for both and I was looking at this as the final stopping point in my career before setting out on my own.

Initially, things were slightly rocky, but went as best as I could have expected. I knew when I accepted the role that the organization was way behind in some of the technology they were using. One of my first duties would be to oversee the implementation of a new platform. One of the reasons I was hired was because I had been a part of implementing a similar platform in prior roles. The implementation project had not been well planned—there had not been a significant amount of change management done around it and there seemed to be very little active support for the pilot phase of the program. The organization did not do a good job planning for and accounting for the changes that were happening within its walls. My tiny team and I were in charge of implementing a new online system with a very short timeline. As the team leader, I thought this was not well planned and when I voiced this to my new boss I was shot down. My team of two was inexperienced in this area and the first phase of the implementation had exhausted them. No one had prepared them for the last-minute changes and pressures that happen with this sort of thing. Worse, it seemed no one had praised them for their success. One of my team members (unbeknownst to me) had applied for the job I received. Within five weeks of my arrival, they quit. The other team member was also going through a lot. My first week there they had a death in the family. No one had coached or developed my team, and they were in personal crisis. I was not surprised when Team Member No. Two gave notice.

Soon after, I met with my boss and offered to resign. I was told the staff changes had nothing to do with me and that they were imminent before I set foot inside the organization. "Shocked everyone lasted this long," my boss said. We decided to look at the staff departures as an opportunity for change. I thought nothing more about the departures on my team, especially when my three-month review was highly positive and encouraging. During my review, my manager seemed very understanding of the situation and even stated that both departures had been a long time in coming. I was not only right on track for my goals and deliverables, but I was exceeding them. I was told I was adapting to the culture well, building relationships, and all in all, there was no question I would be successful. Three months later, it would be a very different story.

A few months later, our department was part of a reorganization. Although we would remain intact as a team, still reporting to our boss, our entire department would be reporting to a new executive leader. Reorganizations such as this are relatively common, notably when there is a new member of the C-Suite. Previously I had been kept out of the regular HR leadership meetings without a reasonable explanation. I had voiced my concerns about this oversight several times to my boss, to no avail. My exclusion from leadership meetings made it very difficult for me to build relationships with other leaders in the department, and it prevented me from learning essential information in a timely manner. When I was finally included in an HR leadership meeting, I thought, *If I am in this meeting, then things must be OK.* I was fooling myself.

Two weeks later, my boss's assistant made an appointment for me to come in to get my six-month evaluation. The meeting was set for 7 a.m. because I "got into the office so early." Clue no. 1: My boss never came in that early. Even though it had been over a week past my probationary period, I knew I wasn't out of the woods. The night before, I stayed up late, deleting my email. Even though I knew there was a digital record, I felt better doing it. I made it a point to dress well for the day—I felt like I was donning armor. I debated taking my car to work but opted for the bus. Maybe that was my last dash of hopefulness.

I arrived as early as the bus schedule allowed and let myself into my office about 5:45 a.m. Methodically, I packed up my things, knowing that an employer cannot look into your private bags if they are closed. And then I waited. When it was time for my review, I walked resolutely down the hall to my boss's office. The admin avoided looking at me. The meeting had been scheduled so early that she had arrived at the office with her hair still wet. I walked into the office, and much to my dismay, I involuntarily gasped at the sight of my HR rep. The presence of my HR rep told me everything I needed to know. My instincts had been right. I was indeed going to lose my job.

My boss and my HR rep couldn't make eye contact with me either. They were well aware of the issues that I had been facing. I received a piece of paper as they fumbled with a clearly canned speech. Although I didn't stop to read the detail of the letter in front of my colleagues, or now-former colleagues, I noticed that the letter was dated one day before my probationary period was officially over. This would mean I would get no severance package, a final insult. What was there to say? All states in the U.S. are commonly referred to as at-will hire-and-fire, meaning employers do not have to give a reason to relieve someone of their position. HR went over the fact that they would cut my access to the online system in fifteen minutes. Both former coworkers looked eager to get me out of the office. My boss, who clearly did not know me at all, asked me if I had any questions. They looked genuinely horrified when I said, "Yes, I wouldn't mind your feedback." I might as well have requested a kidney.

"What do you mean?" they asked.

"Feedback is always important," I said. "What should I take to my next role?"

After a fair amount of fumbling, they started with the generic *It just wasn't a good fit; we decided to go in a different direction* speech.

We all knew why this was happening. I had heard that I had not been my boss's preferred candidate for this role. They had wanted to hire from within but were overruled by their boss. Now, reporting lines had changed. Unfortunately for me, this was a perfect storm of HR being moved to another department and my six-month honeymoon period not having been officially concluded. It all hit at once. I could no longer be protected. I had lacked support pretty much from Day One. Later, I realized I had been allowed to stay long enough for the organizational changes to hit so that my boss could finally hire the person they originally wanted.

Your mother was probably the first person who told you that how others treat you is more a reflection of them, not you. Psychologists and scientists have proven your mother to be a wise woman. When you carry yourself with a high level of integrity and professionalism, more often than not, it inspires animosity. Not that people resent you for your integrity. They resent themselves for their shortcomings. Their only retaliation is to try to find fault with you. As I got up from that table that was much too large for the room, my boss stood up, too. It wasn't out of politeness or professionalism; it was the only way I could have left the room. As I walked by to exit, I held out my right hand. I have never seen a human being look so confused in my entire life.

"What is this?" they asked.

"I wish you well," I replied. Had this never happened before?

After a clammy, too-quick handshake, I looked them in the eye and said goodbye.

Although I was feeling detached from the whole experience, that doesn't mean it didn't impact me. Even though I had seen it coming, that ten minutes in the office felt as if it was happening to another person. The moments after I left the office were among the most awkward moments of my life. They walked me (how humiliating) to my office—sorry, my former office—by the HR rep, who was not happy that my bags were packed. I looked around my office to make sure I had everything I wanted. I saw the dry-erase board where I had so carefully plotted out the team strategy for the year, carefully detailed and color-coded, to let each person on my new team shine and stretch, and I immediately took the eraser and removed it. HR looked shocked and asked me to stop. My HR rep didn't realize that I was removing the last piece of a vision that would never come to light.

As we walked to the door, I mentioned I had no way home. I had taken the commuter bus that day. It didn't provide transportation out of D.C. until the afternoon. It was barely 8 a.m. My HR rep must have felt a subtle sense of integrity or guilt because they went back to the office to request a Lyft to take me home. Noise traveled in our office, and I could hear HR and my now former boss arguing over it. I was being refused this one civility by my boss. I was impressed that HR stood their ground. In the end, HR won. Tiny victory for me. Was a $40 Lyft ride really going to crush the department budget? As the two of them went back and forth, I had the humiliation of watching team members come into the office, each greeting me with a smile—I was well-liked—and then looking crushed once they noticed my many bags. I couldn't help but feel my exit had been scheduled at just the moment for maximum embarrassment for me. I was leaving as people were arriving. HR was set up with a reception area, and I loved the women who worked there. They were tireless and nothing short of delightful. Each one greeted me with a smile and then came close to tears as they saw my bags packed. I had to look away, or else I would also begin to cry. One of my last memories was seeing the face of my newest hire in the tiny glass window of the office side door as he came in. He smiled at me as he went to change out of his travel clothes and into his work clothes. He lived in Baltimore and took a train two hours each way to get to work. I was going to miss him. He was hands down one of the best hires I ever made. HR triumphantly came back to let me know a Lyft driver was coming for me. Because that was going to fix the situation. Luckily, it came quickly as I once again endured the embarrassment of HR walking me to the door so that everyone would know I was *persona non grata*. After I got into the Lyft, my first action was to text my BFF, Lara. I told her what happened, and her response was a classic one-word text: "Bastards." Good friends are hard to find.

I sat in that forsaken Lyft trying to remain calm as coworkers, or rather, former coworkers, started texting me either asking me if I too had received the message to come into the office after 8 a.m. I ignored them. Once I had texted Lara, I allowed myself to cry. Something I refused to do while in the office. My poor Lyft driver. He should have known that it is never a good thing when you pick someone up in a major city and they have their hands full of bags and boxes, and you are driving them 20 miles away at 8 a.m., especially when they are crying. I hope he got a good tip.

I had the driver drop me off at the bus stop in Annapolis so I could get my car. I drove the short distance home, made myself a vodka and tonic at 9 a.m. on a workday, and just sat on my couch in my living room. I think this is how you know whether your job loss is a good or a bad thing. All I can tell you is my first feeling was overwhelming relief. I know of only a few people who were let go from jobs they truly loved, where they felt valued, and where they felt they were contributing. Damn few. I have had that feeling, and I have had those jobs. This was not one of them. All I could think about was that I would not have to work twelve-hour days where I was running to stand still. I would not have to work on weekends. I would not have to put up with the petty politics of the workplace. I was free. I also had thoughts about *How was I going to pay my mortgage and how was I going to pay bills? How was this going to look on my resume?* My situation had become so intolerable that these thoughts were background noise. That is how I knew that in the end, this was going to be a good thing. Somehow.

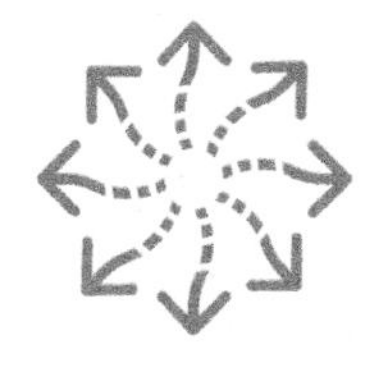

# 1
# THE INITIAL IMPACT OF JOB LOSS

Except for the loss of a loved one or the end of a significant relationship, job loss is one of the greatest stressors we face in life. There are multiple theories as to how to handle the loss. I can tell you from my own experience that one of the worst ways to damage your overall well-being is by downplaying the loss. The demands of challenging jobs and the need to succeed at work set the tone for us to view our lives through the lens of work. We see our coworkers as comrades in arms and maybe even as friends. We look to work to give meaning and purpose to our lives. The feeling of loss is amplified if we are lucky enough to work in an area where we feel a passion or purpose because then we have to fill those holes in our hearts and souls as well as find a new way to earn a living. The pain can be extraordinary and unbearable.

Being out of work is not a finite state. There is a tremendous amount of baggage and activity that comes with it. You go through phases and cycles. No matter how well prepared you are or how you anticipated and planned for it, you are never fully prepared to lose your job. After the actual event, you go through a massive amount of soul searching. It is never a straight line to a new job. We have all heard the story of someone who lost their job, and within a day, a week, or an hour, gets a new and better job. And we despise them almost as much as we envy them. But it is rare. And it isn't always healthy.

I have spent more than a decade of my work life handling, studying, and teaching change management, and trust me, the road to change is never a straight shot-- and if it is, that is a sure sign of trouble. The most successful journeys we take are the unexpected ones and the ones that take us off course. Pivoting from losing one job to immediately starting another isn't normal, and it isn't healthy. You have just suffered a life-altering event. Change is a single event; its ramifications are not. One second, there is a certain reality and the next, there is a new order. The change itself is rarely what trips people up. What scares and confounds people is the adjustment from one "normal" to the next. Think of it as a pebble thrown onto a calm body of water. There is an initial impact, and then, almost out of nowhere, the ripples begin to spread. Sometimes the stone leaves a small indelible wave across the once-calm water, and other times, the rings of water are heavy and go wide and far. An identical pebble can cast different waves depending upon how and where it is thrown, the depth of the water, the weather of the day. Science can probably predict what happens with stones and ponds, but people are not stones or ponds. Your pebble will not cause the same ripple as your friend's or neighbor's. And it will not make the same ripple as the one you threw before or the one you will throw after. People are soft and often unpredictable. What happens after the stone hits the water—after you lose your job—often depends solely upon you.

Work gives routine and structure to our lives. Work allows us to afford the things we not only need but the things we want. Our paychecks will enable us to do the things we enjoy. If we are lucky enough, we even get to enjoy work at a communal level. Work gives us a social outlet not only through coffee room talk but sometimes through company gatherings, contests, Happy Hours, and celebrations. We have a sense of security through our jobs as most of our socio-economic needs are being met. This, in turn, makes us loyal, and in most cases, the better an organization meets our needs, the stronger our loyalty and the harder we work. It is a profound and delicate balance. For so many people, work defines who they are.

Why do we so closely identify ourselves with work? No one comes up to you at a cocktail party or your kid's soccer game and asks, "Who are you?" "What are your values?" No, the first question we almost inevitably ask each other is the decisive question "What do you do?" because that is how we identify and define ourselves. It is our descriptor. *You know Josephine, she's the one who works on the community board.* Or *Lara, the nurse.* We use our work as a means of describing ourselves to others and ourselves. We measure our careers against those of others—*Can you believe I am a Director and Bob, who was class valedictorian, isn't even a manager????* We identify with our titles. We sometimes go so far as to equate ourselves with the companies we work for, adopting their values as our own. *So happy to work for Apple because it shows that I am innovative and creative in everything I do. I am so modern because I work at Snapchat. I am communal and giving because I am at WeWork.*

We define ourselves by our jobs because ever since we can remember, people have asked us what we want to be when we grow up. Can you imagine telling your grandparents that you just want to be a good person when you grow up? My family would have laughed at me. When asked, I always said I wanted to be a doctor. This was to please my biochemist mother and make her think that her child was superior to those of her siblings. When I realized I couldn't handle seeing blood, I switched to saying lawyer because it was just as good. She kept asking me until I was well into my thirties when I would finally go to law school.

It is such a shame that we have yet to instill a value system for our children where we tell them that we want them to be good people and happy. Maybe they would actually grow up to be that way. But we instinctively begin early to define our children and teach them to define themselves by what they want to do. It's just like what was done to us. When a child takes up with paints, his parents say he will be an artist. Why not just say that he will grow up to be creative and able to express himself? When another child is full of questions, we say that she will grow up to be a good lawyer. Why not just encourage her to be inquisitive? It looks as if we may finally have broken that mold by cracking it a little bit with each new generation, as our Millennials and Gen Zers want to be regarded as the people they are, not just by the jobs they do. But that still leaves a glaring number of us who equate ourselves with our jobs, if not our work.

And why wouldn't we do that? We spend more time at work than doing anything else, including sleep. Most of us scoff at the idea of a 40-hour workweek. Does that even exist anymore? We work through lunches, weekends, and holidays. I once worked for a company where the staff referred to PTO as Pretend Time Off. We do all this to try to get ahead. Work colors our moods and dictates our home lives. It isn't a work-life balance (and shouldn't that be a life-work balance? Why do we list *work* first?). It is work, then life, with whatever is left of and for our time and energy. If we are unhappy at work, we bring this baggage to the other areas of our lives. This can stem from the dissatisfaction with what we are doing or with its intensity. Whether we love or hate it, we define ourselves by our occupation or job. It is no small coincidence that many common surnames originate from professions—Baker, Cooper, Smith.

My favorite was a friend of German heritage whose family's original last name was Bauerrisen, which she swore translated to Travelling Farmer.

Job loss is devastating on many fronts. Articles and books often cover the financial burden of a job loss but rarely do people discuss the emotional toll such a loss takes. You can be the best at what you do, and the moment someone removes you from your role, you question your talents and abilities. Why is it that they loved you one day and the next, wanted you to leave? Often, it feels as if you are kicked out of a club or a family.

Psychologists have a term for this morphing of self and work: "enmeshment." The word itself evokes an image of someone trapped in a spider's web, the consonant letters of the word smushing together with only a couple of vowels offering relief, tangling up the tongue as you say it. Enmeshment is when an individual's sense of identity is lost, and instead, two or more people identify as something else, something other than themselves. Individual identity is somehow not as important as the enmeshed identity. It is not the same as the sum being greater than its parts. In enmeshment, you cease to be Robert the programmer for Google but instead identify yourself as a Google employee named Robert. *What and where* Robert is has taken over *who* he is.

When we "enmesh" with another person, we take on their characteristics and feel their emotions beyond common empathy. In true enmeshment, boundaries blur beyond what is appropriate. Whereas in codependency, one person's emotions react to those of another person, in enmeshment, the emotional states are intertwined and do not vary. In codependence, a common reaction to anger is reciprocated anger or fear. In enmeshment, it's a mirror effect.

This is not uncommon. We often seek to identify with a group. We are, after all, social animals and rely upon each other for almost everything. There is a security and a bond that comes from interacting with and relating to others with whom you have things in common. People seek to identify with sports teams, unions, and clubs. Even celebrities have their cliques—Beyonce has the B Hive and Taylor Swift has the Swifties. Joining most of these groups is a safe and necessary aspect of craving and achieving human interaction. Eventually, games end, or singers cease to become popular. More often than not, fans have aged and outgrown teams and entertainers they once idolized. But work and jobs produce a different type of enmeshment. While some organizations give us enjoyment and momentary satisfaction, we put out more than we take. In work, we receive. Work not only provides us with a bond and a brand to identify ourselves with, but work also gives us sustenance and support—not only in the form of our paychecks but in other forms as well. We often look for employers who offer the best benefits when we seek employment. Our jobs take care of us, almost in the way our parents did. They provide money and keep a roof over our heads. They also provide insurance and medical care, education in the form of development, and tuition reimbursement. Work even gives us a sense of identity and worth through promotions and reviews. We come in every day hoping to be noticed and thought well of for our hard work. No wonder people often morph their sense of self with their company. When that identity is lost, we often lose the sense of who we are. The harder and longer we work with a company or in a field, the more we identify ourselves with it.

Even if you have a healthy degree of balance and distance between your work life and your outside of work self, you still initially define yourself by your job. This is one of the reasons it is particularly devastating when you lose your job. It is as if you have lost yourself. Work rewards us with not only money but with perks (insurance, parties, trips), sometimes with praise, and often with friendships, tribes, collectives, and the association with like-minded people. It is very easy to get caught in a web of comfort and security. Companies often like to say that they treat their employees like family.

And why not? Companies often set themselves up as if they were their own country and the competitors are other unfriendly countries. I worked in the insurance industry, and we treated every other insurance company as if they were the enemy waiting to steal our ideas and our clients. We competed with them for every dollar. We even had a team that monitored the news about what our competitors were doing and would announce their failures on our company website. We had a very popular training where we would always favorably compare ourselves with our rivals. I admit that I loved seeing us win. I would report to my students with a sense of pride whenever our company had a perceived win. Once while teaching the class, I received an email from a superior reminding me to tell my class that one of our competitors had just been hit with a major lawsuit and would probably file for bankruptcy. Was I enmeshed with the company or was I just being a good employee? It is a fine line.

Enmeshment can be particularly prevalent for people without a family or a partnership. Work becomes their social outlet. Work can be a place to hide and a place to be busy, to get your mind off of the other things lacking in your life. Work becomes a surrogate for friends and sometimes family.

I'm saying this confidently because it's something I've experienced. I had spent decades learning the craft of what I call Talent Management. In all honesty, I love what I do. I have always been fascinated by the workplace—what makes people choose their professions, what makes them do what they do, how they come together. I love the rules and structure of work and the constant challenge of improving work performance, of meeting employees' and employers' needs. Of aligning goals and strategy and of making things happen. Of making someone's work easier through learning, leadership, and development. There are very few aspects of my work that I do not like, and I have been lucky enough to learn and apply important areas of my work in highly successful organizations. I strongly identify myself through my work and my job. When I set foot in the building Day One of the job mentioned earlier, I knew that the skills and knowledge I had acquired had put me in a position where I would be able to help the organization strategically align its talent management with its vision. I was on the cusp of being a thought leader. I was just a few steps shy of making it all come together. Until, well, you know.

Yes, I felt the impact of losing my paycheck, my insurance, the additional funds in my retirement account. I was saddened by the perceived loss of being unable to continue my education and development. I would miss the brief friendships I had managed to cultivate while there. I missed going to the city each day. I missed getting lunch at the cute little restaurants near the office. I missed watching the tourists walk around. I missed hanging out at Happy Hour after work. But even though I was only there for a brief time, I missed the identity I had worked so hard to create, not only in my field but also with my former employer.

Our work/profession is how we identify ourselves, internally and with others. One of the most significant ways loss of work impacts us is that we lose that identity. One of the main reasons job loss greatly affects our overall feeling of self-worth and confidence is due to identity loss. However, different generations feel the loss of identity in different ways. A middle-aged individual may think that losing their job is a reflection of them not being a valued person. In contrast, someone older (past the age of fifty) might think that their job loss is a reflection of their age or their perspective, their outlook on life or lack of relevance. Even the seemingly indefatigable and resilient Millennial and Gen Z populations feel the impact on their esteem differently. A Millennial might feel a sense "failure to launch." They have had a job but have failed to grab a toehold in their organization or field. They might feel that the job loss is tied to a failure on their part to make an impact, causing them to believe they have come short in transitioning from youth to adult. Millennials often take an early career job loss as an indication that people will always see them as too green, incapable, or even immature. The seemingly irrepressible Gen Z workforce tends to view an early job loss as a sign that what they value (benefits, meaningful work) are not shared by any corporation or organization. Although this does not seem to lead this generation to question their values or what they want from the workplace, it could leave them jaded as to whether or not they will actually find these aspects in a meaningful job.

The "skew" of loss of self-esteem might be different for individuals and our many working generations, but its impact is the same. The feelings of low self-esteem and low confidence tend to increase the longer a person is out of work, regardless of the highs and lows they experience in the roller coaster of seeking employment. Research has found that the degree to which someone feels a crisis of self-confidence resulting from a job loss is not profoundly affected or improved by their surrounding support system. This is often true for younger generations who tend to tie their self-worth to their job. Even when a job loss is imminent based on outside factors such as a company going bankrupt or the economy, most individuals assume that it is somehow their fault when they lose their jobs. (Note that reliable research has yet to be conducted on how individuals who have lost employment due to the COVID-19 pandemic feel about their job loss.)

Loss of identity and confidence are compounded by the lack of daily purpose and routine. Although this seems an obvious assumption, lack of structure and reliable activity significantly affect self-esteem and identity. When a reliable pattern is removed, it increases the feelings of identity loss - the place I used to go to every day is off-limits to me now. It also leaves the body susceptible to conditions that can aggravate the feelings of low self-esteem and low confidence, such as insomnia and anxiety.

It is normal for someone to experience a change in life patterns when going through job loss. It could be staying up later than usual or sleeping in, or even changing eating habits. If left unchecked, continued bad habits can quickly and destructively ravage the mind and body. The path to deeper depression and anxiety is very short, helped along by identity loss and lack of confidence. Without structure and activity, the mind wanders, and most likely, wanders to the dark and obsessive thoughts that come with an adverse life-altering event. If left unchecked, these negative thoughts can take over, causing a few sleepless nights to turn into chronic insomnia, lowering the body's ability to fight illness and the mind's ability to function clearly and optimally. A poor diet can also play havoc with the body's immune system and probiotic health. Comfort eating is a common reaction to bad news. Coupled with a lack of money or energy to prepare proper meals, this leaves the body ripe for sickness, exacerbating depression. Lack of routine is a breeding ground for bad habits that only drag a person further into the realms of stress, anxiety, and depression.

One of the worst realities of unemployment is the lack of security. It is bad enough that we have lost our internal and external identities.

Devastating enough that our self-confidence has taken a hit and that we may feel unvalued or worse, a failure or at fault for our current plight. Our health is now at risk because we have fallen prey to bad habits. We also face the final insult of losing all conditions that generally give us a modicum of safety and security: the steady paycheck, insurance, FSA benefits, retirement savings. The list goes on and on. Worse, there is no way to predict how or when we can begin to rebuild. Most of us who lose jobs are so emotionally stunned by the overwhelming consequences of the loss that it can take days, weeks, or in some cases months for the full impact to be felt and understood. This is even harder to digest because you never know if the storm passing you will be quick or if it will rage on. This uncertainty can make it harder to determine how to handle the storm – and only worsens its impact. All of this can make the future overwhelming. It can leave you immobile, unsure of what action to complete first, and retreating into depression and anxiety for anything from comfort to a hiding place.

But there is hope. Although you had little or no control over your job loss, you do have complete control over how you handle and react to the situation as an individual. You have far more power than you think. How you navigate through the transition and the tangle of emotions and challenges that come with losing your job depends on the actions you choose to take. It's less about the kind of person you are. What follows are suggestions. Go through them at your own pace, doing what works best for you as an individual and for your situation. Just as everyone's pebble toss is different, so will be your ripple from unemployment to returning to work.

One of your first instincts, when you lose your job, is to take some time off for yourself. This is even more tempting if you have some money in the bank (which I had) and your bills are paid up (which mine were). My "enforced" time off came when I had enormous distractions. I was expecting out-of-town guests in a few weeks. I was preparing for a workshop for college students, ironically to help them write their resumes. I had duties as the secretary of my college alumni board to keep me busy. I elected to use the time I would have spent at work to get my place in order for guests and to prepare for the workshop. Initially, this was good as it gave me a focus, so I didn't dwell too much on things and wallow in my situation. In the long run, this was not the best choice.

I have already shared with you that my initial reaction to losing my job was a little time "celebrating" my newfound freedom and binge-watching something on Netflix. These were two things I normally couldn't do because I had been working 14-hour days, almost seven days a week. Another reason I did this was that I was still numb. I had not fully digested all that had happened to me while on the job and after. On some levels, I understood that I was out of work, and had fleeting thoughts of: *What would I do for money?* As often happens with trauma, I had yet to feel and understand the full impact.

In the weeks that followed, I did look for work. I logged on to LinkedIn and Indeed every day. I dusted off the resume that had landed me that dream job, updated a few things, and dutifully sent it on its merry way to the inboxes of recruiters across the tri-state area. I told myself that this was me, focusing on looking for work and finding my new future.

In reality, I spent maybe an hour a day applying for jobs. I started each week with great enthusiasm, convinced that every resume I sent out would be the one to land me my dream job, but as the week wore on, I spent less and less time applying for jobs, and my enthusiasm waned with lack of responses from recruiters. I filled the empty part of my days with TV, half-heartedly organizing my closet, trying the Keto diet, occasionally meeting friends for lunch in the city, (friends I hadn't told that I was out of work) and generally just passing time. I did things I had not been able to do for months. I went to daytime movies. I went to museums. Anything to fill my day. All along, I told myself that my hour a day I spent online applying for jobs would pay off soon, and I would find full-time work, "just like that." After all, the dream job seemed to have come to me with minimal effort on my part. Why wouldn't the next one be as easy? In truth, I was in denial. And I was doing everything wrong.

When you are out of work, finding a new job must be your immediate and top priority. Let me repeat that. When you are out of work, finding a new job must be your immediate and top priority.

Let's explore this a little further. The search varies depending upon your industry, the economy, and your career level, and desired income. I was at an executive level with a six-figure salary. Jobs like that are not very plentiful and my field, learning and development/talent management, is pretty broad. Although there were plenty of opportunities, the titles and salaries were all over the map. And the professional market was fierce in my field and my region. LinkedIn had just added a feature that showed statistical data on applicants for each job listed on the platform. It was not unusual to see that there were hundreds of other applicants to every job I applied for. All of us had advanced degrees and fantastic skills and experience. Due to technology convenience, my fellow applicants did not just live in the Baltimore/Washington D.C. area. They applied from all over the country. Of course, it was not only the job title and position that provoked so much competition. In the District of Columbia, the federal government usually set the bar for salary expectations in the region. Still, companies got around it by having managers do the work of directors and other duties as assigned. Top-salaried jobs were rare. More than one recruiter told me that for every ten thousand dollars you wanted in salary, you could add another month onto your job search. They were eerily correct in my case.

On average, it is supposed to take six weeks to find a job. That is the average, which means the range will be much longer for most of us. *And that six weeks is to get the offer.* If you have recently taken on a new job, you know that between background checks and tiers of interviews, other people's schedules, the occasional drug test, and background screening, it can take another three weeks before your first day.

Let me break it down for you:

| | |
|---|---|
| Time from application to first contact | 2-6 weeks |
| Phone screen | 1-2 weeks |
| Interview, round one | 2 weeks |
| Interview, round two | 2 weeks |
| Interview, round three | 2 weeks |
| Offer | 2-3 weeks |
| Official offer letter | 1 week |
| Background check | 2 weeks |
| Drug screening | 2 weeks |
| Scheduling of the first day | 2 weeks |
| | |
| Total | 22 weeks (approximately) |

All of this can take up to twenty-two weeks (or even more) from when a company receives your initial application to your first day of work. Some of that will depend upon the job level and the recruiting process where you apply for a job. And figure that this is just to get you to the first day. It can take another two weeks after that for your first paycheck. Your first payday is dependent upon how your new workplace pays its employees. I once worked for an organization that paid on the first of each month. I started with them on the fifth of the month, which meant it took more than three weeks to see a paycheck. It might take even longer to start receiving benefits. These are all things you need to consider as you strategize your unemployment period. In retrospect, when I lost my job, I should have made every effort possible to find a job. Later, I will detail about what happens at each step and what you can do to shorten the time between steps. But for now, this should sober you into realizing that when looking for a job you, need to move and move fast. You will find plenty of pockets of free time for family time, development, and any home projects you have been putting off.

Here is my best advice as to what to do first.

## Let it Sink In

If you must, take time off to treat yourself, do nothing. Fine. Do it. But take no more than a day or two. At worst, take a long weekend to lick your wounds. To feel sorry for yourself. To binge-watch *Game of Thrones* imagining yourself as Jon Snow (spoiler alert) coming back from the dead and having the ultimate revenge. But that is it. Let's be realistic about this: You will inevitably have downtime as you no longer will be putting in eight- to twelve-hour days or suffering an interminable commute. You will have pockets of time to go to the gym, to take up a hobby, to spend time with the family, to clean your garage finally. Eventually, I did all of those things. Think of it this way and go back to that high school physics class that you managed to pass by some miracle: *A body at rest tends to stay at rest. A body in motion tends to stay in motion.*

If you completely stop now, there is an excellent chance you will sink into a state of rest. Or worse. If you start to sleep late or through the day, bask in the luxury of afternoon naps, and watch Chandler and Monica get married eight times in a three-month period (thanks to syndication), that pattern is even harder to break. I speak from experience.

My best advice? Take a day, take a weekend. Bask. Wallow. Mourn. But also Plan. Begin to imagine your new Day One. Now you have a new purpose in life: Coming out of this better than you went into it. Again, I speak from experience.

Here is the question that only you can answer: Can you wallow with dignity? In a way, yes. And wallow is a powerful word. I did not initially wallow. I was off to a great start. I binge-watched a show or two, but I also had company for a few days and tons of activities already planned. That saved me, and I regret not continuing with that good start.

As I said, if you want to take a day and sit in your PJs and eat cereal out of the box and binge-watch *Breaking Bad*, go for it. If you're going to take a long weekend of sleeping in and staying up until 2 a.m., OK. But be careful. If you are like me and prone to anxiety and depression, be very, very careful. It can be a slippery slope even if you are not inclined to those things.

I would suggest doing something nice for yourself first when you lost your job. It should not be too extravagant. Make it something that doesn't cost too much and gives you the pleasure your job had denied you. I went to a day movie and met a girlfriend in D.C. for lunch—one of those girlfriend lunches where you order wine and get home at 9 p.m. My job had been silently killing me. I would wake up at 4 a.m. and catch the 5:15 bus to get into downtown D.C. by 6:30. My day was full of meetings, work, emails, answering angry people, and learning. I would work until the 6:20 p.m. bus rolled in, and get home around

7:30 or sometimes even 8 p.m. A quick dinner, and then I was back on email. We had just installed an online performance system for the first time in the company's history. I was not only head of learning and development but also ended up having to serve as the Help Desk for the new system to thousands of people. On lucky days, I would get to bed by 11 p.m. and start the whole thing all over again the next day. I was grateful to be off that hamster wheel, so I did something nice for myself.

One of my biggest errors in looking to reenter the job market was not being strategic. I did what I believe a majority of the population does—I added the latest information to my resume that had gotten me the job from which I was released. Then, I began to blindly click on LinkedIn at any job that sounded remotely interesting and suited my background. I didn't use that sudden gift of time to be strategic and look for something new and different, take stock of my life, or see what changes I needed to make. I didn't alter my old habits a bit as, in my mind, I was going to get a job "any day." I still tried to pay more than the minimum on my credit cards. I bought the same groceries. Counter-productively, I upped my bills by joining a gym to which I never went. I spruced things up around the house by buying furniture and having a few repairs done. I went to dinners and lunches with three-figure tabs. *All because I was sure I was going to get a job immediately.* I didn't, and I ended up paying for it.

Learn from my mistakes. Had I followed this advice, or rather if I had known someone who gave it to me, I would have been so much better off. I could have socked away my unused vacation check to my savings account or used it to pay down credit card debt. I would have been smarter with my money. I took things for granted. Big mistake. Huge.

So, open that bottle of wine, have that lunch, go to that movie, take that semi-lost weekend, but then, be smart. What do I mean by being smart? Be strategic. That means coming up with realistic and practical long-term goals and a way to achieve them. Me, I was in a day-to-day survival mode, foolishly thinking my life would go back to normal. Silly of me because I had no control over that. I had no control over the fact that I was unemployed. What I did have control over was how I handled it, and I did that poorly. Learn from me. I cannot guarantee that you will find a job faster by following my suggestions. I can assure you that you will discover how to utilize time better while unemployed, lessen the chances of making bad choices, and increase the chances of coming out of this predicament better than when you went in it.

## Tell Others

Getting the job that I later lost was one of the pinnacle moments in my career. It's saying a lot because I was already proud of my accomplishments. However, I had considered being offered that job a game-changer for my career. I had intended to use that position as a stepping stone to other things I had always wanted to do: public speaking, being a Thought Leader, writing a book (and no, that irony is not lost on me). Losing that job was one of the most humbling experiences of my life. I felt a combination of emotions it took months to untangle—sadness, anger, failure, grief, disgust, but most of all, shame. I constantly asked myself why I failed. Had I reached too far? What had I done wrong? Why?

I had been fortunate in my career in that so many people I respected thought well of me professionally. And now, those same networks whose admiration was so important to me were going to know I failed. It was more than I could handle, and I did something I'll advise you not to repeat. I barely told anyone of my situation. Maybe it was the shame. Maybe I was afraid that I would hear that I was the failure I thought I was. Maybe I was scared to hear I had gotten what I deserved. I don't know, but whatever I was feeling made me retreat into myself and tell only a few people. And even then, I was afraid of what they might say. I had let everyone down, including myself.

Pride and shame effectively cut me off from the people who could help and support me. Telling my best friend had been a no-brainer. I knew she would be the first person to reassure me it wasn't me but them. I knew I could depend on her as a pillar to lean on and a shoulder to cry on. I told a group of other friends, mainly because they were houseguests, about a week after losing my job and would not see me going to work. These were good friends, and they met my news with a mixture of support and what we all fear, that kind of empathy cloaked in a bit of Thank-God-it-is-you-and-not-me. But to start with, those were the only people I told -- big mistake.

Humans are social animals, and we depend upon each other to survive and thrive. We look to each other for comfort and company as well as to expand ourselves spiritually, professionally, and emotionally. It is only natural to treat a job loss as a personal failure, but let me assure you that it is true in only a few cases. Sometimes things just do not work out. As I write this, the world is feeling the devastating impact of COVID-19. It is changing the way we live, work, and feel. As I do with most tragedies, I hope that we get better from this. This means that we come up with new and deeper perspectives that make us better as humans. I am convinced that the effects of COVID will help us look at work differently. How we work, where we work, and how we look at unemployment and getting back to work. Although the current pandemic-related economy did not inspire this book, I do see the parallels. Current job losses are heartbreaking. This is truly a situation beyond control. But even when we get through this—and we will—I want you to accept job loss as something (largely) beyond your control.

Even when something is out of our control, it still carries a stigma. This is something I am going to ask you to work to get past. As hard as it might be, find the strength to talk about losing your job with your friends, family, and network. Share with anyone you think will be able to help you in some way. In support groups—everything from cancer survivors to Alcoholics Anonymous—members are told that talking about something takes away the strength of what is hurting them and opens them up to receive support. Most people feel the opposite—that if they do not talk about something, they can hide it until it goes away. They are afraid of the shame and the judgment that comes with these situations. When I shared my job loss, not one person ever told me it was my fault. Not everyone was as understanding and supportive as I had wished, and I have learned to accept that. I know this is hard, but find someone, anyone, to talk with about your situation and let others know so they can support you. Because now more than ever, you need that.

The more you discuss your job loss, the easier it will be for you to begin to do the things you need to do to regroup and strategize—the things you will need to do to recover and move forward. The more you put it off, the harder it will be.

## Tell Your Partner and Family

As hard as this is, telling your family should be your first action when you lose work. First, you and your family or partner will have to make plans and critical decisions very quickly. There will need to be discussions about money, insurance, and finances. You might have to discuss child or elder care. You will have to decide upon your priorities, and quickly. For some of these decisions, you will have less than a month.

Do I know a painless and easy way to speak with family or a partner on this? Unfortunately, I do not. I believe these conversations should happen quickly and honestly. Our thoughts of failure and ridicule and not providing for loved ones all make these conversations so difficult. But you will be surprised at how much rallying around a shared foe such as unemployment can bring people together. This is a time to ask your family and partner for trust, support, and help.

Although I have not had to speak to a partner about job loss, I can tell you what it is like from the other side. I have been in a serious relationship where unemployment became the catalyst for ending the relationship. Not because my significant other had lost a job, but because they did not tell me they lost their job --ages after the fact. I felt betrayed and not part of the relationship. I felt untrusted. I wanted and needed to be in a relationship where my partner and I could discuss such things openly. Whether or not my partner realized it, if he couldn't talk to me about those things, how could he ever expect me to come to him if our positions were reversed? Give your family and partner the credit they deserve and have those crucial conversations.

## Tell Your Children

I do not have children, so I do not claim to be an expert where children are concerned. We so often want to protect our children from the things that can hurt them. That is noble and admirable. But children are far more perceptive than we think. They notice even the slightest change of habits and routines. Younger children do not hesitate to ask very open and frank questions. Children are also far more resilient than we assume. They operate far better in the known than the unknown.

I learned this from experience. I was in my teens the first time one of my parents lost their job. My father lost his job and left it to my mother to tell us. Of course, she told my brothers and me not to talk to my father about it. Ever. As dutiful children, we followed orders. For almost a year, we lived in a house where we could not discuss or ask about the most significant event in our lives. My brothers and I somehow knew to stop asking for even the smallest thing, such as money to go to the movies. We didn't question when things got grim—and I mean grim, such as losing electricity for several weeks. We walked around as if we lived in a field strewn with landmines. Predictably, my parents fought often. We were forbidden to tell friends, neighbors, and other family members about our situation, which trapped us in this very uncomfortable environment. As scarring as all of that was, the worst part was that we had no support system for ourselves. I don't think any of us ever recovered from it. Rather than this being a crisis to bring our family together, it ultimately tore us apart.

I am certain that if you thoughtfully and truthfully discuss the situation with your children, you will be teaching them a valuable lesson on how to appropriately deal with certain life's troubles. This is an unforgettable lesson in how character builds us and how we become stronger through adversity. Yes, wanting to protect your child from bad news is instinctive, but showing them how they too can recover from setbacks is an even greater gift to bestow on them.

Just as you would include your partner in major life decisions such as how to budget money, consider bringing your children into the discussion as well. It will prevent them from feeling hopeless and show them that they are helping you because you are making decisions as a family. You will be teaching your children about finance, budgeting, reflecting—amazing skills that will only help them as they get older. Not only that, but you will be building trust with them that will carry over for a lifetime.

## Tell Your Friends

I told friends of my situation on a need-to-know basis, another thing I regret. Some friends, like my best friend, I told right away. Others, such as one former coworker, I told months after the fact. Fewer things let you know who your real friends are than a tragedy. As time goes by, your friends will fall into one of two categories—the people who are your friends are the ones who stand by you, and the people who aren't are the ones who eventually leave you. I regret not telling most of my friends early on. First, because of the need for support and also because I'd have discovered sooner who was really in my corner. I could have concentrated my efforts on the people who truly were friends instead of putting on a pretense for those who were not.

Friends are by far one of the best things in life. These are the people who are with you by choice, not out of obligation or geography. But because they actually like you. They want to be there for you. Letting your friends support you and love you is almost an obligation. They get as much out of it as you do. And eventually, tables may turn. I have friends who were there for me who have since found themselves out of work or in other life-altering situations, and it is my pleasure and, yes, my duty to be there for them.

## Tell Your Network

If you have already built an excellent professional network, you deserve congratulations. Hopefully, you have worked hard to attain a great mixture of industry insiders, former coworkers, peers, and mentors. If not, do not worry; we will get to that later in the book. But if you have, you will now see why you put in such thoughtful and hard work to build this team. Your network exists to support you, educate you, and challenge you. The network guides you. It's there for you to learn more about your field and industry. Now more than ever is the time to put your network to work. When faced with job loss, reach out to your network. Let them know that you are available to them. Let them know that you are looking for a job. Tell them precisely what you are looking for. Ask them to ask friends and colleagues. Make them ask friends of friends and their HR team if anyone can get a suitable role for you.

I have two stories about why it is crucial to speak to your network about your unemployment. My first one is my own mistake. I have a wonderful mentor. I can say without a doubt that she is a person who always expected the best from me but also always supported me. When I left our mutual company to take another job, she was genuinely happy for me. I rewarded her unwavering support by not telling her I had lost my job. I was too ashamed. I was afraid of losing the faith of someone whose opinion I valued so highly. Finally, when I had no other recourse, I told her. As the true professional I knew her to be, she immediately offered to see if there was a role for me at her company. My hesitation cost me, as they had already filled the position. But through that lack of faith, I realized that she wasn't just my mentor; she was also my friend. As much as it cost me, I would take that trade-off any day because she is a fantastic friend. I just couldn't see it at the time.

My second story ends on a much more successful note. When we think of using our network, we need to think of the degrees-of-separation theory: How many degrees of separation are you away from who you need to know? My friend Matt saw a job on LinkedIn that he knew was perfect for him. He realized that he did not know anyone in that organization. Rather than give up, he reached out to his entire network on LinkedIn and asked if anyone knew anyone who worked there. He has been happily employed there for over a year. He made the network work. You should too.

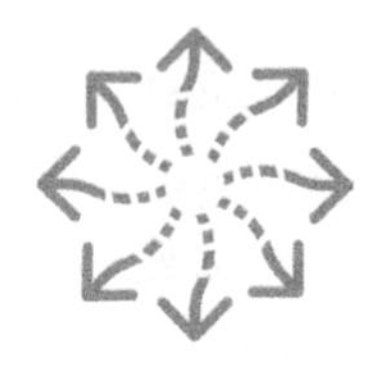

# 2
# PIVOTING AND PLANNING

Look at searching for your job as a job. You are the CEO of *You, Inc.* You need to treat yourself like a bona fide organization. You will need to keep an eye on your budget, expenses, maintenance, goals and strategy, and staff (that would be you and sometimes, your network). You will keep track of your time. You will take care of all of your resources—including YOU! You will make sure that your employee (You, again) has a proper life-work balance. If you run yourself and your job search like a well-organized company, chances are you will have an extremely efficient and effective job search.

## Finding Your Niche

I work in a fascinating field. I loosely refer to it as talent management, but it runs the gamut from human resources, learning, to change management. A big function of my work is to help people and organizations determine their goals and the strategies for reaching them. This is important because, without a plan, it is virtually impossible to reach your goal. This is how I want to help you reach your goal of finding a new job.

Your job hunt should be a strategic process. You may be tempted once you lose your job to jump right in and search. That is what I did, the hypocrite that I am. I got home that day, threw something on Netflix, poured a drink, and promptly started applying to any job that sounded reasonably passable. Why? Because I thought that was what I should do. What is worse was, I continued to do this, month after month. And yes, sometimes it even worked. In the midst of all the applications, I got an occasional interview. But in the end, it took me almost a full year to get a new job. It was only when I stopped being tactical and started being mindful and strategic that my results changed for the better. Almost overnight. I want to save you the time, heartache, and money that my lack of insight and planning cost me. I had never been out of work before. And it was a scary and lonely experience of trying to traverse the unknown. I didn't know what to do beyond trying to find a job. I want to help you navigate through this and to learn from my hard-earned experience.

You may not realize it, but by losing your job, you have received a gift. You have just been handed the rare opportunity for a significant change in your life. It comes with a feeling of helplessness because this is not a change you necessarily sought; it was thrust upon you and probably not welcome. But it is the opportunity to reevaluate, assess your life, your wants, needs, and to determine what direction you should take. It is an even rarer privilege to evaluate your life and career choices to find out that, yes, you made the right decisions after all or utilized the opportunity to change course. I want you to do what I failed to do. I want you to learn from my mistakes – all of them. I want you to

use this opportunity to rework your professional life. What better time than now?
One of the first things I want you to know is that you are not alone. Remember the parable of The Hole. Recently, I had the privilege of speaking with Andy Storch, host of the *Talent Development Hot Seat* podcast, about his own experience with a career not working out. In addition to hosting the podcast, Andy runs the Talent Development Think Tank and is the author of the book: *Own Your Career Own Your Life*. As of this writing, Andy's book is the number one career guide on Amazon. Andy reached out to connect with me on LinkedIn after securing a job with a global company. I have to admit I was flattered because, from the outside, it looked as if Andy really had all the answers and had led, at least professionally, a charmed life. When I connected with him about my book, he shared his own job loss story with me. Andy was doing quite well at a firm that offered leaders learning solutions to their educational and strategic goals. Andy was sincere that although he loved the job, it did not wholly fulfill him, and he wasn't good with some of the job's aspects and where his performance was below his expectations. When he eventually failed to get a long-coveted promotion, he left the company. He knew his career had reached its peak there. He was disappointed, but he looked at it as the opportunity he needed to commit to his consulting business fully. He has not looked back since.

## Reflecting on Your Career

You are at a crossroads. Maybe you are one of those lucky folks who always knew what you wanted to do for a living. Or maybe you were like me and lucky enough that someone saw something in you and guided you to the perfect career for you. Perhaps, you just aren't sure. I could point you to a hundred assessments all bent on helping you learn about you and your likes and dislikes, your aptitudes and abilities. And they might help guide you, and it is always interesting to learn about yourself. But no one knows you as you do. This is the time to reflect and decide: What to do with your life?

This is your time to rethink You and your path. As Andy said, not getting that promotion did not define him. He did not look at leaving his company as a failure but rather as a sign that he should do something else. He realized that his former job had three pillars: consulting, sales, and programming. He excelled and enjoyed two of those pillars—sales and consulting. He used those two loves and skills as the foundation for his own business. Andy is much happier, and it shows. I have met few people who enjoy what they do more. And this is precisely why people connect with Andy—he has an enthusiasm and love for what he does that makes you want to work with him. Just as Andy found his purpose, I want to help you harness yours. One area to start is to reflect upon You and what You stand for.

When at a crossroads (and I want you to look at losing your job as a crossroads), Andy suggests taking time to reflect. Ask yourself key questions: *Are you enjoying what you are/were doing? Does it bring joy to you?* Think about what you want for your future career path.

How do you go about this if you aren't as lucky as Andy?

I love tying real life to pop culture. There is a movie starring Hilary Swank where she is left a very young widow. With the help of family and friends, she fights her way out of depression at the loss of her husband and is able to resume a new life. Part of that is figuring out what career she should pursue. In the best scene from the movie, she is in her living room surrounded by flip chart-sized lists with different likes, passions, and possible job ideas to help her choose a career. My favorite is the list that starts with Vampire Slayer.

Eventually, the combination of her love of designer clothes and her artistic talent leads Hilary's character to pursue a career as a shoe designer. It is a movie, so naturally, everything she does is beautiful and successful, but the point is, she actually takes the time to find her passion and talents.

Make sure that you end up doing something that speaks to your passion and talents in this time of change. In his masterpiece, *Great at Work*, Morten Hansen writes that people need both purpose and passion to be successful at work and feel fulfilled. This can come in many forms. You can genuinely enjoy your career as an accountant. However, being a CPA for the IRS and being one for Amnesty International appeals to the passions of two very different people even though they have the same purpose. This is the opportunity to explore your skillset and your passion. What makes your soul and heart sing? Are you happy with your career choice but just wish you were doing it better or for a particular type of company?

There are a few resources to help you decide what truly makes you happy, or rather, what you need to make you happy. Believe it or not, science has proven what people need to be happy. The University of Pennsylvania offers a free Authentic Happiness Inventory tool, https://www.authentichappiness.sas.upenn.edu/, that helps you learn what you need in your life to be happy—which goes a long way to combining purpose and passion. No job or situation will give you all of the factors you need to be happy, but you can cross a few of them off your list once you have identified them. I took the assessment while I was unemployed. I found that learning and constant improvement are high on my list of happiness factors. Given my field, that was not exactly new information. I didn't need this inventory to prove that I was in a career I was well suited for, but it was nice to have that affirmed. The assessment told me that to be happy, I need to be surrounded by beauty, order, and integrity. That goes a long way in helping me determine the type of organization where I want to work—and now, the kind of organization I want to build.

Other things you can look at: What are your other career paths? Vampire Slayer or shoe designer? What transferable skills do you have that could take you to another field? I was fortunate when I made my major career change—a recruiter saw I had a learning professional's core skills, even though that wasn't in my background. I had worked in HR and for the company where the recruiter worked, which went a long way toward establishing credibility. I was a good communicator. I was organized. I am a consummate planner. I had a genuine love of knowledge and learning. Margaret, the recruiter who changed my life, helped me take my passions—learning, leadership, structure, organization, love of the workplace—and bring my existing skills and experience to a new career.

When I was hired, my new boss told me that she and the team felt they could teach me the hard skills I needed to do the job, even though I had very little learning and development experience. They were hiring me for the qualities I had that could not be learned. Looking back, I realize how lucky I was that I was given this career path. Most of the time I get so excited about my work. I love that I help people make their work-life—where they spend most of their time—a better place. I get to help people solve problems. I help people feel good about themselves, and I help them develop for new opportunities. Most of the time, my job does not feel like work to me. I see the benefits and results of what I do almost every single day. I can spend more than 40 hours a week on what I do. I took my latest role because I was so taken by one of the leaders in the department. When he offered me the job in person I had asked him why they had selected me. He seemed a little taken aback, but without hesitating, he replied, "Because you have a tremendous passion for what you do. We need that here." He was right. When looking for work, it never occurred to me to look for something in another field. I know my purpose without a doubt. Take the Authentic Happiness Inventory to find yours.

## Is This the Time to Further Your Education?

Part of being strategic is being aware of what you need to move to the next step, especially if you are changing paths. For the record, in the movie, Hilary Swank's character managed to carve out a career just by attending a few classes in design at the local learning annex. You will probably need to do a little more education than that. Whether you are forging a new career or just augmenting the one you already have, you should always look at developing yourself professionally and personally. Now is the perfect time to do this as you have that elusive gift of free time. This is another area I could have done better in while I was out of work. Instead, let me share with you the success story of a colleague of mine.

A couple of jobs back, I worked with Henry (name changed at his request). We both worked in learning for the same organization but in different departments. I worked for the parent company, and he worked for a smaller company that we had recently acquired. In the smaller company, Henry had been promoted to the role of director and let me know every day that he felt he was above me in the pecking order because my title was "Head of. . ." and in his opinion, not as high as his. Worse, whenever I asked him to work on a project to help with something, his manager let me know that he was far too busy. Finally, I got him to work on a presentation for me and was shocked at how amateur it was. It was full of typos and misspellings, misalignments, and incorrect work. More distressing than anything else, this presentation lacked any tenets of adult learning. It was just information placed on a slide deck. When I spoke with him about it, Henry said that they never tried too hard on internal work because it was just for the employees.

I informed him that those might have been the standards of the former organization, but the parent company requested that anything you did be high-quality as if you were presenting to the CEO because every employee here had equal importance.

I had to coach Henry, and I often suggested improving his skills by attending a program that taught adult learning theory and concepts. From then on, Henry ignored me. Over a year later, I left the company, and someone else was tasked with helping Henry improve his work. Henry's response was to quit. About six months later, Henry's former boss reached out to invite me to lunch, and while catching up, he let me know that Henry had enrolled in the same program I had once suggested. I reached out to Henry and asked him to lunch, and when we met, he told me, "Now I finally know all those things you had been talking about!" Henry is now in a new job, and his enhanced skill set has allowed him to approach it with a new passion. I had not realized that Henry's stubbornness at work was because he was self-taught. He didn't know how to fix his weaknesses and was scared that they would be visible. Now that you have the opportunity, this is a time to take stock of your work and your skillset to see if anything needs to be improved or learned before you return to the job market.

One of the often-underutilized blessings of unemployment is the free education most states offer if you receive unemployment benefits. They are not always easy to find, but they are there, and most of them are free. You will have the privilege of having access to most of them the entire time you are unemployed. In most cases, your educational benefits will run for a full calendar year, starting at the date of your unemployment registration. In other words, even if you are lucky enough to find employment quickly, there is a chance that you will still have access to free educational resources. Each state's offerings vary.

Your educational benefits are based on your state of residence, not the location of your former employer. For example, I lost my D.C. job, and I lived in Maryland, so I was only entitled to the Maryland education benefit. However, this was not a time to be shy. I have always wanted to get a specific HR certification but never found the time or felt I had the resources to pay for the courses or the testing. I discovered that Maryland offered the SHRM certification as a benefit of unemployment, as did D.C. However, I could not track down a program owner in Maryland. Since my unemployment benefit was through D.C., I contacted my rep there for advice. She couldn't help, but a couple of weeks after I contacted her, she had had someone in the D.C. office send me the link for free courses because I had been so persistent.

In our COVID-19 environment, many colleges and universities are offering free online learning or at a reduced cost to people who have lost their jobs because of the pandemic. In addition, sites such as Coursera and LinkedIn also offer free education, even if you are still employed. These are fantastic opportunities. Do not let them go to waste.

Let's assume that you have roughly figured out the career path you want to take by now. It is time to carefully decide what your reworking will look like. First, let's decide what you "stand for,"—Brand You—and what your career would be in a perfect world.

## Mission and Vision

One thing that great organizations have in common is a fantastic mission and vision statement. Few organizations differentiate between the two, and more often than not, it is just a good slogan etched in the glass behind a reception area. Good companies, actually great ones, have a well-thought-out and empowering mission and vision. They not only live it, but it becomes embedded in the fabric of everything they do. Some people call it an identifier; some call it a brand. Whatever you call it, you first have to determine what it is, which is why I suggest you create yours. I am the number one supporter and consultant for You Inc., and one of our first tasks is going to be to make sure you have a proper mission and vision for your search.

Let's get straight what sets a mission and vision apart. A mission statement is just that—it tells people what Now is. What are you doing? Your vision is broader and maybe a little more abstract because it defines the future or desired state.

Mission answers the key questions, such as:

- What are you doing?
- How are you doing it?
- Who is it for?
- What is your immediate intent?
- What is your purpose?

The mission statement will be your credo, your battle cry, the thing you say to pick yourself up when you are down. It should motivate and excite. It should direct. It should push you to meet your goal, no matter what. In other words, a lot is riding on the mission statement.

Companies pay consultants and employees thousands upon thousands of dollars to craft the perfect mission statement. Months and months, sometimes even years, go into designing and developing the perfect mission. Focus groups are held. Surveys are sent. Drafts are written and rejected until, hopefully, the perfect sentence is formed that best describes the Now.

It can be a little overwhelming. Luckily for you, the process can be straightforward. Also, where an organization has to please tons of people both internally and externally, you only have to please yourself. Make sure that you do.

To motivate you, here are some top mission statements from some well-known companies and organizations:

**LinkedIn:** *"To connect the world's professionals to make them more productive and successful."*

**Amazon:** "*We aim to be Earth's most customer-centric company. Our mission is to continually raise the bar of the customer experience by using the internet and technology to help consumers find, discover and buy anything, and empower businesses and content creators to maximize their success."*

I particularly like **Kickstarter's:** *"To help bring creative projects to life."* Simple, to the point but still with an air of magic to it.

**Google,** proving that a mission should reflect the organization completely**:** *"To organize the world's information and make it universally accessible and useful."* On the surface, Google is a company with a simple task—as its mission states. Its logos use primary colors and the company's name. Underneath, it's a different story. Initially, Google followed and met its mission. It became one of the earth's most-used search engines despite a crowded field at its launch. It was useful and accessible to all. Well, as long as you could get onto the internet.

Mission statements should be long-lasting but change as the needs, identity, strategy, and goals of an organization change. But above all, mission statements should be simple and straightforward. You should know what exactly the mission is. Although Kickstarter's mission statement is a little imagination-based, you still know that it is an organization that wants to help people bring their dreams and ideas to reality. Mission statements that are too long, too complicated, and leave you scratching your head are bad.

**Albertsons:** *"To create a shopping experience that pleases our customers; a workplace that creates opportunities and a great working environment for our associates; and a business that achieves financial success."* From this, you have no idea what they sell or what constitutes a great workplace in their mind. And it is a little self-serving to have in your mission statement that you want to be financially successful. You're a business. We kind of assumed you'd want to make money.

Another example of a self-serving mission statement is from **MGM Resorts:** *"MGM Resorts International is the leader in entertainment & hospitality—a diverse collection of extraordinary people, distinctive brands and best in class destinations."*

Don't ever say you are the leader in your mission statement. It can come back to haunt you. Instead, they could have put something along the lines of *"Leading entertainment and hospitality through diversity and distinction across the world."* This would have shown their desire to lead an industry and set the standard on multiple levels, through the people they employ and the guests they serve. Clearly, MGM did not consult me for their mission statement.

## Writing Your Goal or Mission Statement

Now back to you. I am asking you to create a mission statement for your time out of work. This is to be about how you will handle this time of unemployment. Crafting the mission statement that will get you out of bed each day is incredibly easy. I think you will find it more than a little empowering.

First, start with something generic:

*I want to use this time to discover what exactly it is that I want to do for a living and to obtain a job at my needed income level that leaves me rich and fulfilled.*

Then think about the specifics of what you want from your career search:

- What do you want to do?
- How are you doing it?
- Who is it for?
- What do you stand for?
- What do you value?

Answers to your questions might be:

- What do you want to do? *Land a leadership role.*
- How are you doing it? *Leveraging my learning and healthcare background.*
- Who is it for? *Me and my students.*
- What do you stand for? *Creativity, improvement, altruism, world peace, humanity, individuality.*
- Where do you want to work? *Global organizations with a sense of service, good inclusive and collaborative employee environment.*

Your revised first-draft mission statement might be:

*Combining my learning and development background with my healthcare knowledge to land a leadership role in an organization that works to make the world a better place, one person at a time.*

I came close to this when I got my last job. This may sound like a silly exercise but by the time I got around to doing this, reading my mission statement each day reminded me what I was looking for. It made me focus only on talent management jobs at companies with a global reputation and social conscience. I wanted a learning role that allowed me to be creative and use my talent. I stopped applying to any job and started to apply for The Job. It forced me to recognize what I was looking for, search only for those things, and not settle for less. It inspired and kept me focused.

You don't have to keep your first draft. You can keep honing your statement to match the job market or as other areas of interest crop up. You can revise your mission statement as you learn more about yourself and the type of career you want throughout your job search. The important thing here is to have a starting point to properly prioritize and focus your efforts in your job search.

If you are struggling with adjectives or verbs for your mission statement, treat it like magnetic poetry or Mad Libs. Write out the statement with blanks and a series of "suggester" words:

**Use my education to ________ a job in the ___________ field for a major _______ company.**

**Suggester words:**

*Find, secure, land, get, create*

*Research, literary, educational*

*Manufacturing, design, aeronautics*

Play around with the words and sentences until you feel comfortable and confident with your mission. My favorite example of this was my client Sophie (name changed at her request). She struggled with this until she had friends over for dinner. Someone saw the skeletal sentence on her bathroom mirror and insisted no one leave the party until the group had helped her complete her mission statement. Their collaboration helped her to home in on a career as an esthetician (a hidden desire of hers). Often the best statements are written by a committee. So, if you are struggling with this, ask for help. Do not let perfect become the enemy of good. Have your family or friends help you draft your statement.

You are the CEO and HR of You, Inc. Go ahead and hire yourself some interns.

Once you have a mission statement that inspires you, post it where you will see it often. Post it in large print. Say it multiple times a day. Say it before logging online. Say it before job interviews. Say it as you meditate. Say it before you go to bed at night. Never forget your mission.

## Vision

While the mission is what you stand for. Now, the current state of You, Inc., your vision statement is where you want to go. What is your ideal, future, ultimate form? Where do you want to be eventually? I am tasking you with writing both a mission and a vision statement because I want you to rethink looking for a job. Do not think of getting a job as your eventual destination. Even if you are fortunate enough to land your dream job right away, it will be essential that you keep learning, growing, and evolving. To do this, you must not only know the immediate need but the eventual one. The vision is your direction, your purpose, your unconditional, perfect world state. Know that you might not achieve it, but you have no hope without setting your course. By setting your course, you embrace hope. A lack of vision is just you living from day to day. And we both want more than that for You, Inc.

Writing a vision statement is similar to writing the mission statement, you might need to reflect a little more on this because the vision statement is your idea of perfection. With the mission statement, you knew that looking for a job was Priority One. You might not know your ideal future state, and that is OK. But it is never too soon to start thinking about your perfect world. Start with these questions:

- What exactly do you want to do?
- What problem (yours, the world's) do you want to solve?
- What cause do you want to support?
- What is the change you want to be?
- Why is this so important?
- What is your Why?

In his fantastic book, *Start with Why*, Simon Sinek points out that people and organizations with a higher purpose and calling not only have a greater chance of being successful but also a greater chance of retaining their success. This is because their action follows their purpose. According to Sinek, your "Why" is your calling. Do you want to change the world? Do you want to help others? Do you want to save lives? Knowing your "Why" impacts the things you do. As you think about your "Why" statements, think beyond making money or achieving fame for yourself. Those things should be secondary. Instead, think about how you want what you do to impact your well-being and the well-being of others. For example, do you want to have a hand in lessening global poverty? Do you want to be a role model for your family? Do you want to change the way people think about something? All noble "Whys" is a great start for a vision statement. Once you understand what makes you passionate, you can begin to determine how you will achieve it.

A vision statement reflects your values and dreams. It helps you direct your course. It aids you in making important decisions (such as which job to take). Whereas your mission statement might change depending upon the phases of your career, the vision statement stays relatively the same unless your ultimate desire changes. Whereas mission statements are grounded in the real world, vision statements are not. They should have a hint of the fantastical and impossible about them.

Mission statements help you achieve. Vision statements help you dream. Mission statements are achievable. Vision statements are almost inconceivable or unobtainable. But above all, vision statements should be something someone wants. Some top vision statements include:

**Oxfam:** *"A world without poverty."*

**Nike:** *"Do everything possible to expand human potential."*

**Alzheimer's Association:** *"A world without Alzheimer's disease."*

Who doesn't want a world without poverty or Alzheimer's disease? Don't most people want to expand their potential? Because this will be a Vision statement for You, Inc., the Vision should be what you want for yourself, for your career. One of my favorite examples of why mission and vision statements are so important comes from Sinek's book. He tells the story of Samuel Langley. Langley had a well-funded venture that, in part, was supported by the deep pockets of the U.S. government. He had skilled teams on his side, the best equipment, and plenty of opportunities. But when the time came, he failed miserably at his chosen task. His motivators were not noble. He wanted to be the first to do something magical, but his motivators were fame and fortune. Worse, he gave up after his first failure. Shortly after Langley's failure, another small group tried the same venture. They were poor. They were unskilled. However, they believed in the magic of what they set out to do. More importantly, they looked at adversity as a learning experience, and rather than being daunted by each failure; they used it to modify their plans and attempts. And so, on December 4, 1903, the Wright Brothers achieved what is considered the first official flight of man. I like to think their mission was merely, "*To fly*" and their vision: "*To take man beyond the earth.*" The only limit to your vision is you.

Once you have a mission and vision, like any successful organization, you will need to plan for how to get there.

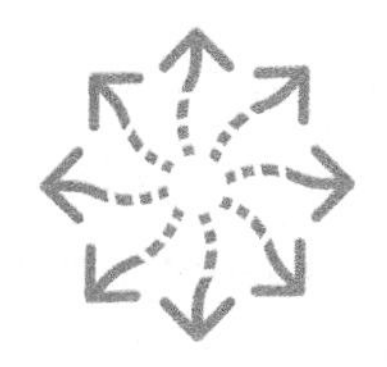

# 3
# GETTING YOUR HOUSE IN ORDER

When you lost your job, you also lost your routine and structure. It is very easy to slip into a tactical mode of doing one thing after another with little purpose or connection. I want you to think of getting a job just as you would think about a work goal—to get there, you not only need to have the goal in mind, but you also have to come up with the strategy of how you are going to get there. You need to treat finding a job like a job unto itself. What is your objective? What is your plan? What are your deliverables? What are your obstacles and potential roadblocks? Having all of this in place *before* you start looking for a job will go a long way to ensure your success. One of the first rules of being strategic is looking at your mission and determining what it will take to get you there. What do you need to complete your mission successfully?

You do not need formal training to figure out a successful strategy for finding a job. This doesn't require a project manager certification, but it does require reflection and brutal honesty. I would also recommend doing this in a quiet spot where there are no distractions. In my initial job search, I went from task to task with no order and no direction, and I paid the price on many levels.

My lack of proper planning and strategy cost me financially. But more importantly, it cost me time in my job search. Remember our calculations: **Eleven to twenty-two weeks away from that first paycheck.** You cannot afford to waste any time with those stakes, but you can afford to strategize. First of all, you have this book as an aid. However, it's more about common sense and approaching things thoughtfully. One of the easiest ways to plan is just one small step beyond your garden variety To-Do List. Besides writing out all that you think you need to do in your job search, you should group common things together—often called bucketing—and then prioritize each bucket, so you approach and complete it sensibly. There is no right or wrong here, and it is highly personalized. Initially, I did not bucket items. I didn't even have a plan. The process that follows will ensure that your time of being out of work will have a minimal negative impact on you and your family. Your buckets and how you prioritize the items in each bucket will depend upon your needs and your situation. Only you can make that determination.

There is a resource section at the back of this book to help you get organized. For now, let's look at some potential buckets in detail.

## Common Strategy Buckets

- Immediate needs
- Family
- Health
- House
- Job search
- Car
- Money

## Obstacles

- Bills
- Lack of a job
- Distractions
- Transportation

## Dependencies

- Money
- Financial obligations
- Health insurance
- Mental health
- Finding what I want to do
- Family obligations/ family needs
- Car

The first thing to do is to take stock of your current state. We wrote your mission statement, and now we have to make sure that the current state is in shape to focus on your goal of getting a job. One of the first things successful organizations do after a huge event or before setting a strategy is to take stock of everything—budget, resources, needs. That is what we are going to do. Admittedly, this part is tricky. But as hard as it is, you have to know the truth to build a successful plan. You might be afraid—of the future, of not having enough money, of things being worse than you thought. But knowing is better than not knowing. Ignorance is not bliss.

The hard and sad truth is that life as you and your family have known has changed, and you have to adjust accordingly. Maybe you were lucky, and you received a severance check. Maybe you have unpaid vacation time coming your way. Perhaps, you have some money in the bank. Count yourself among the blessed few. The reality is that you will have to make some immediate lifestyle adjustments and make them right away. I am not going to be a complete killjoy here. Yes, go out to a nice dinner if you can. Or splurge on a good bottle of wine. Just don't overdo it.

This is an area where I hugely failed and faltered when I was unemployed. If I had taken action on a few items first, my period of unemployment might not have been so difficult or costly in the long run. I have to admit that I have been very blessed in life. I used to tell people that you could say a lot about me, but the one area in life where I was always sure of myself was that I would always be able to earn a living. For the past two decades, I have worked very hard in a field I love to amass a diverse background. Where most people in my field specialized, I diversified. It was always how I answered the question: *What sets you apart from others interviewing for this role?* And it almost always worked. I was able to diversify in my field, and also trade up in organizations and roles. Not an easy feat. On the plus side, this chameleon quality served me well. I have always had multiple job offers. Until a little while ago, I had never been without a job. The irony of this good luck is that when I found myself out of work, I had no knowledge or experience in handling being out of work. If you will, I was a failure at being unemployed because I didn't know what to do or how to prioritize my actions. But the good news is, now I know what to do if this ever happens again. And I am now sharing this knowledge so that others do not have to make my mistakes.

What follows is a group of suggestions. Feel free to follow one of them or all of them. The order will depend on you and your needs, *but I suggest you do most of them within the first two weeks of losing your job.* Some of them are time-sensitive, such as using your FSA card and healthcare benefits. So is filing for unemployment. Most of this is hard. It is humbling, and in some cases, humiliating. I found it to be so. I felt like a complete failure and, in some cases, a deadbeat as I filed for various types of unemployment assistance -- another mistake of mine. Assistance programs exist for a reason—to help people—and right now, you need help. You will be OK in the long run. But for now, take every bit of help and assistance available to you. Keep in mind, in most cases, you are looking at being eleven to twenty-two weeks away from a paycheck. Now is the time to act.

## (Unemployment) Life Hacks

The meaning of the word "hack" has had a fascinating history. Originally it meant *grind* or *servant.* It morphed into meaning either someone who was cut-rate or incompetent. In the past decade and a half (thanks to the tech culture), *hack* has come to mean a trick or a method to gain efficiency. It might be slightly outside the box, and it might not be conventional, but hacks are meant to save us time, effort, money, and maybe even a little heartache. They make our lives better. What follows are the unemployment hacks I learned while out of work. They served to save me time, money, and certain heartache. I had to learn them the hard way—through trial and error. There were lots and lots of errors.

**File for Unemployment.** Before losing my Dream Job, the closest I ever came to unemployment was when my government contract ran out. I had filled out my unemployment paperwork, and then before I needed to file, I suddenly had three job offers. So, according to my experience, I would be OK when I lost my job. I had no intention of filing for unemployment. My rationale was that I would certainly have a job within six weeks, and I had enough in savings and PTO (Paid Time Off) pay coming to me that I wouldn't need to file. In reality, I didn't get a new job within six weeks, and the tiny nest egg I had from my unused vacation pay ran out. Rather than file, I dipped into my retirement account (mistake). It was only when all my other resources ran out that I realized my error. To make matters worse, I didn't realize that not only was there a deadline to file for unemployment but, there is also a delay in getting your unemployment pay. You can stop laughing at my innocence anytime. But not everyone knows this, and you wouldn't know unless you have been unemployed before or unless you are close to someone who has been. Unemployment programs and processes vary from state to state. Even though I lived in Maryland, I received D.C. benefits as that was where I had worked. This is also significant because each state or district has its own rules about calculating the amount a participant gets and also the time they are on benefits. In D.C., the limit was ten weeks. In Maryland, you can put in for an extension. In D.C., you cannot. Lesson learned.

How you file for benefits and how you send weekly updates also might vary. For D.C., I was able to do everything online, which made the process easy and convenient. D. C. residents who don't own a computer can do everything over the phone. At the time, in Maryland, if you couldn't file your unemployment online, you had to go to your area unemployment office to file and to give weekly updates on your employment search.

It took about two weeks for me to start receiving benefits. The first week was a "test" week, meaning I did not receive unemployment pay; so technically, it was three weeks from the date I initially filed before I started receiving actual money in my account. Some states have agreements with major credit card companies to run debit card accounts for beneficiaries. Once weekly benefits are approved, a dollar amount is loaded onto a debit card in the filer's name. Once benefits begin, this is very convenient for the recipient. Not everyone has a bank account or the ability to access one. However, opening the initial debit card account can take up to four weeks. If you were already living paycheck to paycheck, that could feel like a lifetime. As you can guess, the amount was not staggering nor really near my usual paycheck, but it was money coming in. They are your benefits—use them.

**One more note:** You will probably have the option of having taxes deducted from your benefits. That is a personal decision. I opted to have them taken out as the dollar amount seemed nominal, and I didn't want to worry about that at tax time. If you can afford to, consider this option.

**Apply for Food Assistance/Supplemental Nutrition Assistance Program (SNAP).** I didn't even think about food assistance until things got truly desperate on my end. I ran out of food and started googling agencies and food pantries in Maryland. Food assistance/SNAP came up in my online search. I applied and was pleasantly surprised that I qualified. I received almost $300 a month in benefits. For a single person willing to be creative, that was a fortune. All it took was going down to the state office in Annapolis, sitting for an interview, and filling out some paperwork. The waiting room was packed. I later found out that most people were there to renew their annual benefits. In my state, your benefits are for a year, and then you need to interview again. It is a pretty straightforward process. SNAP benefits have moved into the modern age where you can order groceries online (even through Amazon or Instacart). You will have to check each merchant's website as their instructions are unique, but this is an incredible lifesaver if you cannot leave your home due to child or elder care. Or if getting to a grocery store is difficult.

In truth, I should have applied for SNAP benefits the second I lost my job. I was indeed eligible. Although I had no problem paying for groceries for the first six months I was out of work; I didn't have to. It was a benefit for which I qualified. And it would have been an additional $300 or so a month I could put to other bills. To put it in perspective, that was about the same dollar amount as my car payment.

Although SNAP benefits are a federal program, each state runs its own SNAP program. In Maryland and most likely all other states, anyone is free to apply for this benefit. An application does not guarantee approval. I found the process painless and relatively quick. I had my Independence card within two weeks of being approved for benefits. This link can help you apply in your state and even provide some details on the process as well as any restrictions in your state: https://www.msn.com/en-us/money/personalfinance/where-to-apply-for-food-assistance-in-every-state/ss-BB13MRlV?li=BBnb7Kz#image=1. Even though I was receiving D.C. unemployment benefits, I had to apply for SNAP benefits in my state of residence. Make sure you know the rules to save yourself some time and worry. You can also get tips on how to use your SNAP benefits on the Feeding America website www.feedingamerica.org. Also, look into local food pantries and child nutrition programs, which vary from state to state and county to county, as well as WIC (Women and Infant Children) programs. Most of these are detailed on the Feeding America site. Do not discount local churches and other organizations. Now is not the time to be proud. These programs exist for a reason. When times are better for you, think about giving back—be it as a volunteer or in the form of a donation.

It took very little time for me to receive my Independence card from the state. It looks like any other bank card/debit card, and most grocery stores in my area accepted it. Every month like clockwork, they automatically loaded money onto my card. Occasionally I received a letter from the state asking me to confirm my eligibility, which I dutifully returned. Other than that, it was a pain-free process. **A small word of warning: You can't buy everything at a grocery store with your Independence card.** Personal hygiene items usually are not part of SNAP benefits. If you use this benefit, look for specific labels on grocery shelves that indicate if a product is SNAP eligible. You will see the acronym SNAP on the shelf price label (not the label on the food product) that lets you know you can purchase the item with your card. This can be a lifesaver if you have no extra money to cover any unpaid balances.

Another thing I appreciated was the lack of judgment from store clerks when I used my card. No one even acknowledged it, except for my favorite cashier at my local grocery, Miss Charlotte. When she noticed I was using a SNAP card, all she said when she handed me my receipt was, "Bless you, Honey, things are going to go your way soon." I cried on the way home in the car, touched by her discretion and humanity.

**Obtain Insurance.** Insurance is one of the scariest issues when you lose your job, especially if you have a family or an ongoing medical condition. If a company is worth its salt, someone in HR will talk you through an off-boarding or separation process. That is a very polite way of saying that they let you go properly. In most cases, you will be handed a slew of papers (or emailed them) that read like IKEA instructions. And it is scary. The idea of not having medical care causes almost as much anxiety as no longer having a steady paycheck.

Federal law provides people who lose jobs the right to continue purchasing healthcare for a limited period (often three months) through their former employer, commonly known as COBRA (Consolidated Omnibus Budget Reconciliation Act). Your employer's plan no longer covers you, so you can rejoin the plan as you no longer work for the company. There is a certain irony to it. By law, you should be notified of this option upon release from your employer. Like most things, some companies do this better than others. Some walk you through all of your options. Others hand you or mail you the paperwork, and you are left on your own to figure it out, or you can contact a third-party benefits center. The thought of filing and paying for COBRA can be overwhelming.

There are a few things your former employer might not directly tell you about COBRA. You have no obligation to rejoin your former employer's health plan. You have other, often more affordable options for your healthcare. As I write this, the Affordable Healthcare Act, or ACA, requires all Americans to have medical coverage, with a few exceptions. If you do not have healthcare coverage through an employer, spouse or parent, the ACA requires you to purchase your insurance at surprisingly affordable rates through state-run exchanges. Because it is part of your former employer's healthcare plan, COBRA can be pretty expensive because you pay both your share and your employer's portion of your insurance. In addition, in most cases, you only have the option to have COBRA for a limited period. *Keep in mind that if you work for an employer for even one day of a month, your employer covers your insurance for the entire month (provided you were on their insurance plan).* This means that if you were let go on the first of the month, you would not need to purchase insurance until the following month. This will become important later. But for the moment, you wouldn't need insurance immediately.

Healthcare was another hiccup of my unemployment journey. I could have and should have applied to the exchanges right away. Had I known how valuable and necessary the benefit would be for me, I would have done things differently. Medical care was my big concern while unemployed. I have a chronic health condition, anemia. It requires iron infusions every six weeks, along with bi-monthly visits to the phlebotomist and a hematologist. I was able to get in one last round of treatment before my insurance ran out at the end of September. After that, my primary form of treatment was prayer until I joined the exchanges.

I had waited until December to get any type of medical treatment, mainly because, I didn't think I needed it aside from the iron. The December after I lost my job, I realized I needed a flu shot, I went to my primary care physician. I knew I would have to pay the "regular" rate but thought that I had plenty of money on my Flexible Savings Account (FSA) card, which I thought I could use until the end of the year to cover the cost. I was wrong. At the doctor's office, they informed me that the card wouldn't go through. Thinking it was a technical glitch, I asked to be billed, which they did. When I got home, I called the customer service number for my flexible spending account provider, where I learned the hard truth. My FSA benefits ended at the end of the month I was last employed—September. I was not happy about that. I ended up paying over $300 for a flu shot I could have gotten for free at any one of numerous clinics in the area.

Because of the time of year, I was inundated with TV commercials about applying for insurance on the exchanges. It was the law and ACA registration follows the calendar year unless you have had the aforementioned life-altering event. According to the Affordable Healthcare Act, unless you met the exception criteria for enrollment (coverage through a parent, spouse, etc.), you had to be privately insured or insured through your state-run exchange. If not, you will be breaking the law, which would result in your tax refund being garnished. Most people who are not insured by their employer or are unemployed tend to get at least a little something back from their state and federal governments at tax time. That is one of the reasons refunds are garnished if offenders are not registered for the ACA. As I was hoping for a nice refund, I went online and applied to the Maryland exchanges. A reminder: Because of how the U.S. government is structured, things like unemployment, food benefits, and healthcare are all managed on a state level, even though they are federal programs.

The ACA exchange for Maryland was also done online, although there were options to go to a center and have someone walk you through applying. I chose to apply online. Much to my surprise, the system was easy to navigate. It fell short from a consumer point of view because I didn't quite understand my registration results and following up was arduous. When logging on to the state exchanges, applicants answer several questions regarding medical needs, location, family and household, and income levels. All information is used to determine which coverage options applicants qualify for. From there, applicants can choose from a variety of insurance plans based on the coverage they need. Major medical insurance companies offer all plans such as Cigna, Blue Cross/Blue Shield, etc. It is very similar to choosing a plan offered by an employer. Once an applicant selects a plan, they set up billing arrangements through the insurance provider (not the state exchange). The applicant receives their new insurance card in the mail and should use the plan criteria when meeting their medical needs. It turned out that despite my former income, my current state of unemployment meant that I qualified for Medicaid. Being on Medicaid meant that I did not have an insurance provider per se but was on a state-run program. Since I applied in December, I did not technically qualify for benefits until January. I received a paper card in the mail and very little instruction. I only had to show the card when I needed care.

Little did I know that I would be putting that to the test sooner rather than later. In mid-February, I felt sick. I think this was a combination of being depressed and scared over my job and income situations, genuinely being sick, and having just lost a plumb job for which I had been interviewing for over three months. I went to my local urgent care, thinking my regular doctor was too far geographically (no gas money) and that I could no longer afford him. I didn't know how much I would have to pay based on what Medicaid didn't cover. I was diagnosed with walking pneumonia. The doctor told me that although walking pneumonia usually goes away on its own, my case had seriously progressed. I was shocked but grateful when my little Medicaid card covered all of my urgent care visits. I only had to pay $1 per prescription. My concern that I couldn't pay a medical bill would ultimately result in my being bedridden for almost six weeks. This is a decision that millions of Americans make every day, and I suddenly understood why. My greatest joy at leaving the center that day was realizing that I could indeed get medical care when I became sick while out of work.

Because losing my job was a qualifying life event according to insurance companies, I could have registered on the exchanges in September and been covered from October onward. Another mistake I made that I urge you not to follow. This is not the time of pride but the time of action. I was so lucky and grateful the ACA existed while I was unemployed. The good news is that it looks as if this federal mandate will be around for a few more years. If you cannot afford private insurance or COBRA, go to the exchanges and apply. You may be surprised by what you are offered.

One more note about insurance. Most providers do not let you switch plans or change your benefits during the year unless you have had a life-altering event such as a birth in the family or a job loss. This can be critical to you and your family if all of you are on your plan, and your partner's company also provides insurance. Under those circumstances, most companies will allow your partner to place you and your family on their plan. You will have to show proof of the change, but it is a straightforward process in most cases. However, it is time-sensitive and should be one of the first things you investigate after losing your job.

Chapter 3

# Money

Money is a very tough and touchy topic. But oh, so necessary. I was not smart with my money. And as I got further along in my unemployment period, I spent more and more time in my house. I spent weeks if not months, cooped up in my house primarily because I had no money to do anything. I was terrified I would get a job interview and not have gas money to get to it—which truly happened. Don't let this happen to you. Here are a few things to do to get your financial house in order.

**Take Stock of Your Money.** Find out how much money you have. Maybe you are lucky and have a nest egg. Thank goodness I did have that. Maybe you even have a retirement account. Let's park that item. Hopefully, you will get a severance check. Not everyone is in that position. I was not. One of your first assignments is to find out how much money you have. Bank accounts, savings accounts, wallets, coin jars. Mark down anything that is an asset. Start a spreadsheet. List your assets. Do you have something that needs to be returned to the store or credited back to a credit card? Take care of that now. Do you have bottles to go to recycling? A rebate for something? Now is not the time to be proud. Now is the time to be proactive. Don't forget to assemble any gift cards, metro cards, etc., you have lying around the house. You will need them. We will discuss budgets later.

**Assess and Use Healthcare Needs and Assets.** Let's do a deeper dive into your healthcare beyond the issue of insurance. You've just lost your job, and very few people can afford COBRA. I'm not even sure why they have it. Keep in mind that you do not have to sign up for it right away. It is like a safety net and there for when you need it. If you are offered COBRA, find out the deadline for filing for your specific package and use this date as a guideline for making your other healthcare choices. As of this writing, the Affordable Healthcare Act is still in effect, so by law, you will need insurance. I will write more about this later, but you will not get arrested or taxed for missing a month of insurance. The government has bigger concerns. My worry for you is your immediate healthcare needs. For the remainder of the month, your insurance from your old job is still an asset. Some employers still have hearts and let employees go early in the month to remain insured as long as possible. I have also noticed lately that some companies are paying for their employees' COBRA. I find this to be extremely generous as they have no obligation to do so. Take advantage of your former employer's generosity! My former employer did not offer to pay my COBRA and let me go halfway through the month. But I still had insurance.

**Refill prescriptions.** Check your prescriptions, and stock up because you don't know when you will be insured or what your new insurance plan will allow. Call your doctors and let them know your situation. Ask for refills on your prescriptions and get them filled. Ask for more medication than you usually receive. Be mindful of all your ongoing health issues. For instance, if you are let go in January with spring and pollen season coming up, call your doctor and let them know what happened. Get your medications up to date as soon as possible.

**Make appointments with all your healthcare providers.** See your doctors, your dentists, and your eye doctor. If you are like me, you only went to the doctor if a bone was sticking out because work kept you so busy. Immediately make all those neglected appointments. If doctors will not or cannot see you, let the receptionist/nurse know that you will not have insurance at the end of the month. Do not back down. I was let go in mid-September. I spent the last two weeks of the month in doctors' offices. Not because I was sick, but because I needed checkups and tests and prescription refills. Whenever I let the office know I was going to lose my insurance, they give me an appointment. My OBGYN books very early. It is usually a three- to six-month wait for an appointment. When I told them my situation, I had an appointment the next day. I am so grateful to them. If your regular doctor will not or cannot see you, ask for a referral to another doctor or find another one through your provider. But make sure the doctor you see is in your network and takes your insurance. And I repeat—do not forget your trips to the dentist and the eye doctor. I got in my final dental cleaning for the year and an eye exam. I also stocked up on contact lenses. Even if you do not feel you need to prioritize your medical care, don't forget the rest of your family! You have a clock running on this issue. Do not let it run out.

**Use your FSA and HSA accounts.** Unbeknownst to me, my FSA card was no longer valid beyond the end of the month in which I lost my job. I naively thought that my FSA went to the end of the calendar year, and after losing my job in September, I tried to use it for an uninsured doctor's visit in December. That mistake cost me $300. Use up every penny of your FSA before it expires—buy over-the-counter medications you will need, pay off any doctor's bills. Whatever it takes. *The issuing employer keeps unused FSA dollars.* You do not want to leave any of that money with your former employer. Do the same for your Health Savings Account and dependent benefits. Rules and restrictions may vary from plan to plan. If you have questions, be insistent that someone from Benefits or the company that manages those accounts for your former employer speak with you immediately. Time is not on your side, and you need to make immediate decisions. You do not want to leave money on the table.

Now that we know the essential resources for You, Inc., let's take an even harder look at budgets and money.

**Cut Your Expenses.** I was lucky and a little spoiled. I had finally reached that point in my life where I had stopped looking at what came in vs. what went out as I was able to stay on top of my bills. I had even managed to pay down credit cards and save, and it at least felt that I was living well within my means. My semi-charmed lifestyle was very short-lived, and I got knocked down a peg or two. Take an honest look at your budget. Do not quantify, round down, or justify. Just write it down. And this is not like your weight on your driver's license, so don't fudge. Be very, very honest about your monthly bills and your debt --every little thing. Don't forget your Amazon Music or Audible subscription. Or that wine or clothing subscription. Do not forget the gym you never visit. Do not forget the wine subscription, etc. You will be shocked at what money is leaving your bank account.

Once you know the intake and the outgo, see where you can trim the fat. This is another area where I could have done better. Remember, these are your monthly bills. You have just lost your income stream. Even if you have the nest egg and get a job right away, it is not going to hurt you to cut back. Seriously, you will be amazed at what you can live on. You will be shocked at what you can trim and at how spoiled you had become. Besides, when you get that new job, you will need to focus on it. All that background noise will rarely get used. Suppose you do manage to come out of this ahead. In that case, you can use that extra money to take a vacation once that new PTO kicks in or give your family a lovely holiday and celebrate that you not only survived unemployment but that you thrived in unemployment. But if your time in unemployment is lengthy and your bank account becomes lean like mine became, you will be better prepared to weather the storm.

Things you can probably cut back on:

**Dining Out.** I dined out way too much, and what is worse, I tried too hard to keep up with my friends who had jobs and to continue the illusion I could still keep my old lifestyle. When I was employed, I often picked up the tab for friends, proud that I had the income to do so. My error was continuing to do so after I lost my job out of fear of telling people the truth and the desire to keep up appearances. A few friends treated me to meals out, and in the end, I needed them to treat me. If you choose to go out as your occasional treat, here is my best advice: Pick a dollar amount you are comfortable spending on a meal. Find the best restaurant in the area in that price range and either take yourself or your family out. And then very, very judiciously choose your dining out options during this period of unemployment. But do not dine out as if you still had a job. You will be shocked by how much you used to spend on takeout and dining out. If you want to meet friends, that is fine, but no rule states you have to meet for dinner or a pricey brunch.

Do not forget to include little dining out items that add up quickly, such as your daily latte or smoothie. Have one once in a while as a treat or to celebrate something but as part of your routine, make beverages at home and get a reusable travel mug or thermos. My friend Mary and I regularly met for coffee once a month. It was our treat as well as an important social/support need for both of us. We were both out of work, and the staff at our local Panera was well aware of our work situation. The manager would even give us free cookies, which we were not too proud to take. While she and I both were watching our wallets, we also agreed that our monthly meetings were essential for our well-being because they provided us both with a social outlet. They also gave us the chance to check in on one another.

**Streaming Services.** There are so many free streaming services these days that you can go without a paying streaming service and still find plenty to entertain you. You can obtain most free services online. If you are unsure of this one, consider asking your provider to pause your service for a few weeks. You won't even miss it.

**Video games, movie rentals.** The cost for this can pile up for adults and children alike. I suggest cutting this out entirely due to the distraction and cost. Children will find other activities to fill up their time. As a parent, you can help them do that. And adults, well, for now, put things on hold. Again, you might be surprised how much else you accomplish by cutting this out of your life.

**Memberships.** Clubs, gyms, different organizations. This is one to think about very selectively because, at some of these gatherings, networking also happens, which can be a blessing when out of work. Carefully ask yourself if you are using your membership and if it is helpful to you. I did not use my gym membership despite good intentions. It was money out the window. However, I did belong to a professional group that I found invaluable while out of work. While my gym membership went unused, I met with my professional group weekly. We helped each other solve work problems, supported one another, and even have a Slack job board. In addition, connections I formed with the group helped me acquire multiple consulting jobs, which provided me a small income stream while still giving me the flexibility to focus on my job hunt. You don't have to give up all your memberships; just make sure that you are receiving value from the ones you keep. Cutting back on distractions will allow you to focus on yourself, your family, and the job hunt.

**Subscription Boxes and Monthly Subscriptions.** Subscriptions are designed to make money for a company. You can get almost anything through a subscription box. The trouble with most subscription boxes is most people have a tough time keeping up with the items they receive. If you receive one or more subscription boxes, you probably have enough wine, cigars, skincare, or whatever else you have received to get by for a while. Monthly subscriptions are another expense you can probably live without. Do you need that magazine? How is having a monthly music subscription adding value to your life? Are these items want-to-haves or have-to-haves? You will be amazed at how much you are spending when you add it up. This was one area where I excelled, and I managed to cut over $150 a month on subscriptions. I have not gone back to most of them.

**Amazon and other online shopping.** Here is an exercise to stop your heart: Go to your Amazon page and look at your order history for the past year. Breathe deep. But yes, it is probably as bad as you think. We are living in a time of immediate gratification. Kick your online shopping habit. Going to the store will ensure that you are purchasing things you need, help keep the planet safe, and save you money. If you don't trust that inner impulsive shopper in you, then shop at stores that will shop for you and let you just pick it up. It will get you out of the house and seeing everything in one bundle will make you realize how much you do and don't need.

**Gym membership.** This is a tough one. If you can establish a healthy routine and use this regularly, it might be worth keeping. That is if you go. I had good intentions and did not take advantage of my membership. Eventually, I canceled it and instead took my walks in the local park.

**Donations.** This was a hard one for me. I had gotten to a place in life where I felt I could give back. I donated to my college and practically anything Bono told me I should support, as well as any international disaster. I helped friends who were down on their luck. I gave to the local shelter, and even sent anonymous money to a few students at my alma mater. Most of the time, I had these amounts automatically deducted from my bank account. I continued doing this through most of my unemployment until a friend read me the riot act about needing donations myself. I had to stop taking care of others so I could take care of myself. One of my proudest moments, after I went back to work, was restarting most of these donations. For now, stop trying to save the world, at least with money. When you get back to work, you can go back to being Bono.

**Automatic payments.** We live in a world that prides itself on making our lives easy. I cannot recall the last time I spoke with anyone at my bank or wrote a check. I have automatic payments come out of my account for most of my bills. This saves time and effort. I do not have a large online footprint. Still, I am proud that if you Google my name, one of the things that comes up is that my student loan holder had me give a testimonial of how I was able to pay off my loan so quickly and with no penalties. I owe it all to automatic payments.

The drawback of automatic payments is that sometimes we forget them. We go on autopilot. This is how I continued to pay for a gym membership for a year after I thought I had quit it. Go through all of your automatic payments and see if there is anything you need to stop. See if there is anything you can and should decrease. Before I lost my job, I was obsessed with getting out of debt quickly and paying more than the minimum payment on credit cards through autopay. When I looked hard at my post-job budget, I reluctantly went through card by card and took everything down to the minimum. You should ruthlessly go through all bank accounts and all credit cards to ensure that any autopay transactions are valid, up to date, and justifiable.

Now that you have taken stock of what needs to go out or stop going out financially, think about what you need to keep. Here is some practical advice for some things you need to decide:

**Credit cards.** Because I was still trying to get out of debt, I continued to pay more than the minimum on my credit cards, even though I lost my job. This was not a smart move on my part. I should have immediately began paying only the minimum on my cards when I lost my job. I didn't. I had a false belief that I would get a job any minute, so why change what I was doing? But none of us knows the future. Upon losing your job and income, you should immediately pay only the minimum on your credit cards. In today's online world, you can easily change back to paying more on your cards when you are financially able to do so. The reality is that your income has been severely compromised, and you need to act accordingly. If you are not sure what to do, there are many resources available to help you.

Maybe you were lucky enough to have requested financial planning through your former employer, or better yet, they offered an Employee

Assistance Program (EAP). You should have access to the program through the end of your last month of employment. Most people believe an EAP is only for mental health services, but EAPs are versatile and offer resources on everything from marital counseling to party planning. Even a solid hour of advice from a financial planner is worth using to help you get your house to weather the storm. Consider online resources as well. For example, Experian and other credit score tracking websites offer solid financial management advice to customers who find themselves low on funds and unable to meet their financial obligations.

You may be worried about a high-interest rate on a card racking up fees and debt while you are out of work. And that is a genuine concern. My strategy suggestion is to have you minimize the amount of money going out so that you will continue to have as much disposable income as possible and to be able to at least pay the minimum payment on your debt. This will keep your credit score stable while you look for work.

The truth of the matter is that any credit card company will work with you. They want you to be able to pay your debt. If you walk away from it, declare bankruptcy, or default on your debt, it isn't good for either of you. If you truly get in a bind, you can call your creditors and ask for a payment holiday without incurring interest in most cases. But do this proactively before you have to miss a payment, not after you are late with one. Companies are more apt to work with you when they don't have to chase you down. Some companies will offer to reduce your interest rate, usually based upon your track record as a customer and your overall credit score. Or they will let you skip a payment. American Express made me that offer. But, and this is the hard part, **you have to ask.** It is scary and can be very intimidating, but it's worse to jeopardize your credit score or available credit that you might have to access for an emergency.

**Loans.** Only you can decide whether or not to take out a loan. If your credit card debt is high, you have probably already received offers for consolidation loans. The idea is that the loan interest rate is much lower than the average interest rate among your cards. You get the loan and use it to pay off your cards and then pay a smaller amount to the lender than you would have paid to your credit card companies. This might work if you had a steady income. Otherwise, there is enormous temptation to take the loan and bank the money for household expenses. The problem with this is that you don't know when you will get a job, and now you have just doubled your debt size *and* have an additional payment to make each month. Only you can decide if this risk is worth it—or if you can pay off high-interest credit cards with the loan amount you receive. Tread carefully here.

**Family Activities.** This is hard because I am counting things such as children's lessons, sports, etc. We love our families, and we want to give them everything they want and need. I can imagine few things as difficult as telling a child that you can no longer afford for them to do something that brings them joy. The reality is that if there is a cut in income, there needs to be a lifestyle change. This might include your child's soccer program or violin lessons. Understandably, this may be one of the last things you cut from your budget. You should at least take a look at this to see how you can lessen the expense. Maybe you can help coach your child's sports team for a reduction in their participation fee or find a less expensive alternative for music lessons. At the very least, examine the expense regularly to be sure you can still afford it.

Although your child may be disappointed that they have to temporarily give up a cherished activity, having a mature and honest discussion with them about it will make them feel included. It will teach them a valuable life lesson of how to make choices appropriately. Having a frank conversation will also make your child feel they have a say in this matter—that it is a sacrifice they are making by choice rather than having it thrust upon them. They may even feel that by giving up a particular activity, they are contributing to the well-being of the family.

**Childcare/Elder Care.** Caring for others is at the same time a privilege and a burden, financially and emotionally. If you normally pay for regular dependent care, I suggest you continue to do so if that is at all feasible. I understand that dependent care is going to be one of your biggest expenses and that, on the surface, you (and perhaps others) will think that because you are not going to work each day that you will have the time and freedom to care for others, but that is not the case. Being out of work is an enormous stressor. Looking for work and caring for yourself at the same time is arduous and time-consuming. You will need minimal distractions and interruptions to apply for jobs, write resumes, interview, etc. As you cannot plan everything on your job search, you will need guaranteed free time. If your finances are stretched, I suggest keeping your dependent care in place for at least two days a week. This way, you will have two known days for interviews, errands, and most importantly, yourself. Think of the oxygen mask speech from air travel: Before you help anyone else with their mask, you must first make sure that your own is secure. If you don't take care of yourself, you cannot take care of others.

If this argument does not convince you, here is another. Often programs for childcare and eldercare have waiting lists. At least the good ones do. If you opt to have your loved one stay at home with you full time, consider the burden it would place on you to find a new facility for them once you have a job. The last thing you want is to get a new job only to have to push back your first day while you search for dependable, safe care for a loved one.

If your resources are stretched indeed, discuss this with the facility. I had one client who was a former teacher's aide. She arranged to volunteer one day a week at her child's daycare in return for a lower weekly fee. She got to spend quality time with her child and still had free time to look for work. Make sure the facility that cares for your loved one is aware of your situation. Ask them to work with you. Maybe they can defer payments or help you come up with a payment plan. You never know unless you ask.

**Cars/Transportation:** If you have a car note that you are paying, you need to prioritize this. Your car is your way to job interviews, and once you get a job, your way to work. When I was out of work, I feared losing my car and religiously made my car payment. I did manage to screw up the courage to call my lender and ask what my options were on my car payment. This is a little harder to wrangle than asking a credit card company to come to terms, or even your mortgage company. A car rarely holds its value. As you pay off a car loan, you are in a race of time to pay off the loan while the car's value keeps pace with the car note. Often, you end up with a note on the car that is always slightly more than the car's Blue Book value. Lenders are usually willing to discuss things—at least, mine was. Lenders are in the business of lending money, not selling used cars. Mine was willing to give me a payment holiday, but at the cost of huge surcharges. In the end, I decided it wasn't worth it and kept paying for my vehicle. Luckily, I was able to do that.

I also suggest giving your car the once-over. Luckily, I had a mechanic who was willing to look at my car for potential issues, and while I still felt flush, I did things such as replacing a tire, air filter, and an unreliable starter. The last thing you want is to be without dependable transportation. You might have to stretch out the maintenance on your car—and with you not driving it to work every day, this should be feasible—but you want to be prepared prepare for any repairs that might have to be needed.

**Pets.** While you are getting your house in order, do not forget those wonderful creatures who bring us joy and unconditional love. If you have been putting off getting your pet to a vet for a checkup or shots or even a nail trim, do it now. You do not want your pet to suffer because of your situation. Don't forget to stock up on any of their supplies—food, treats, shots, and medicine. As with other hacks I have mentioned, I would do this for at least three months. I would not resort to giving pets people food unless it's an emergency. Switching up your animal's diet can cause digestive distress, and then you will have an unexpected and potentially expensive vet bill. If you have a pet that requires grooming, add that to your budget, so your beloved friend does not suffer. Postponing grooming that dogs need is unhealthy for them. Such neglect can lead to serious medical issues such as blocked glands and infected nails and paws. Keep up with their care.

If your pet is lucky enough that you hired them a walker or sitter while you were at work each day or even took them to daycare, consider putting all of that on hold. Your pet loves you and being together brings both of you joy. Besides helping your mental well-being, having to care for a pet, especially one you have to walk, will help keep you moving and give you a sense of responsibility to keep you on track in your search for work.

Besides covering the day-to-day aspect of getting by while unemployed, it is crucial to make sure you are ready for the unexpected. Think of the Scout motto, "Be Prepared."

**Clothes/Emergency Interview Kit.** Why is this important? Earlier, I mentioned having a job interview and not getting to it because I didn't have gas and toll money. Things got that desperate. I want to be sure that does not happen to you. This is the kit that will have you ready for a job interview at a moment's notice, no matter what is in your bank account.

First and foremost, you will need something to wear. Depending upon the job level you are applying for, you may need two or more things to wear. One job I interviewed for involved four separate in-person interviews, and yes, interviewers talk to each other, and mention if you are properly dressed. For that particular interview set, I recycled the black interview dress that I had worn at the first interview for the final interview. I accessorized it differently and wore a different jacket. I thought that was fine until I was leaving the building and ran into someone from my first interview in the elevator. She was kind and gracious and just as I was leaving the elevator, commented that she had liked the black dress from her interview with me and wondered where I had purchased it. I was humiliated. No, I didn't get the job.

Here is my best advice for you: Put aside at least two suits/interview outfits—three if you can swing it and if you are applying for a leadership or executive role. In today's casual work-from-home environment, it is hard to have interview-quality clothes at the ready, so you may no longer have appropriate clothing on hand. If that is the case, go out and purchase something. Think of this as an investment in yourself. If you have been in a job for a while, the suit that got you your former job may no longer be in style, which will be very important as you sit for an interview. It's understandable if you do not feel you can afford a new interview outfit or two, so borrow from an understanding fashion-forward friend. Or get creative and check out sales, Goodwill, and organizations such as Dress for Success. You will feel relief and confidence knowing that you have interview clothes ready. Look for things that are made of year-round fabric. I suggest dark-colored clothes, which give an air of business and seriousness and look good on everyone. Also, err on the conservative side. If you have an interview at a more casual or creative organization, you can always give the nod to that with the shirt or tie you add to the suit. Men sometimes like to do this with socks. Also, make sure you have the proper accessories—jewelry for women, ties, and socks for men. Make sure you have a nice un-scuffed handbag (sorry, but women can be judgmental with each other on this one) or laptop bag if you carry that with you. Don't go too flashy on this. I had a client want to borrow her sister's Birkin bag to take to a job interview at a nonprofit. I spent an hour trying to talk her out of it. Amid lots of tears, she argued that the bag gave her confidence. I told her that such an extravagant bag sent the wrong message. It virtually screamed, "I don't really need this job, and I am better than you." She took the bag with her, and later, much later, she received an unofficial feedback that the organization felt her values were not aligned with theirs. She gave her sister back the bag. Gather your ensemble for the most common denominator.

In addition to your interview clothes, put together something to wear for your first day of work. As your tenure in unemployment grows, you will never have as much money as you do right now, so this is the time to make a smart and purposeful splurge. You want to make the best first impression and have confidence on your first day of work. Be prepared.

Don't forget to include money in your Emergency Interview Kit. This is one of the hardest things to remember because of course, every penny is precious. I suggest tucking away a nice crisp twenty in your suit pocket or your handbag. This is an updated version of mothers telling their children always to have an emergency quarter for a payphone. Cash is always good to have if you are in an interview and need to grab a snack or a paper to read while waiting in a coffee shop. It is also good for putting gas in your car, buying a MetroCard, etc. A super-smart way to go is to purchase gift cards for these items. I preferred this method so that I wasn't tempted to spend the cash on a depression pizza or an out-of-my-price-range latte. I tucked a gas card, a full Metro pass, a Starbucks card, and a Visa gift card in my interview handbag. They came in handy more than once.

**Interview Preparation Kit.** Here is a list of the things you should have ready:

- One or two dark-colored suits
- Blouse or shirt
- Appropriate shoes, buffed, polished and ready
- Socks or hosiery
- Jewelry (here is where you can be a little creative and let your true self shine)
- Tie (for men)
- Bag/laptop bag

And just in case:

- Professional rain gear (trench coats never go out of style)
- Umbrella—work-appropriate, please, something that collapses easily for convenience
- and something in a solid color. If you only have something with a logo, make sure it is subtle. Probably best to leave your sports team umbrella at home for now.
- Winter coats if needed, including gloves, scarves, etc.

Make sure everything is clean, pressed, and ready. I took everything to the dry cleaners before I assembled my kit. If it needs repair, it is not ready -- no holes, runs, or stains. Check everything in full sunlight. Store your kit appropriately, away from moths, tobacco smoke, and if you have children, curious hands. Make sure your kit is not crowded in a closet or wherever you hang it so that you will not have to iron things at the last minute. I kept my kit on a rack in my spare bedroom and checked on it once a week. After an interview, I immediately washed it or freshened it in the dryer with a dryer sheet and then hung it up.

The idea is that everything is always ready for you. When you are called for an interview, and they want you to come in immediately or schedule an impromptu video call, you can do it confidently because you are ready. Even if you don't get that last-minute interview call, your kit will be waiting for you. It falls under the *Better to have it and not need it than need it and not have it* category. I occasionally changed accessories as the mood struck me or as the seasons changed. Knowing that I was ready for anything allowed me to focus on preparing my facts for an interview and avoiding rushing the day of looking for run-free hose.

Make sure your clothes fit and try them on *regularly* - once a week should be sufficient. The less-than-active lifestyle of being unemployed caused my size to shift—another thing I did wrong. If your suit feels a touch snug Monday, cut back on portions and take a daily walk (both will do you good) until it fits better. If you are one of those people who can regularly get to the gym or exercise (kudos—I respect and envy you at the same time), you may need to trade your suit in for a smaller model, but you don't want to learn that the day of an interview. A floppy suit does not reflect professionalism.

**Keeping Your Style.** Access to style essentials such as razors, clippers, products, and the money needed for a last-minute haircut is part of your Interview Kit. I do not want to come off shallow here, but let's face it, we live in a world where appearances count. This one is so much harder on women than on men, not only from an emotional level but also a financial one. We live in a world that has a double standard. A man can go to a job interview with slightly longer hair and stubble, and he is considered bohemian or even a little avant-garde. He is hip and cool. Men can also brush their teeth and put on a tie, and they are James Bond. It isn't fair, but there it is.

Women, on the other hand, well, there is a standard, and I lived it. When I was employed, despite working twelve- to-fourteen-hour days, I still managed to get my hair colored every month, get the monthly mani-pedi, and have my eyebrows waxed. I was spoiled. Monthly pampering was my one indulgence. I also considered it essential. As an executive, I was expected to look a certain way. I even managed to get monthly massages and quarterly facials. I upgraded my makeup from L'Oréal bought in a drugstore to Dior bought in a department store. At least for a while. Another mistake I made after

I lost my job was keeping my routines. I justified them in that I would get a job any minute and needed to be appropriately groomed to give the right impression. After six months of trying to keep up with my former self, I learned to back off. I learned to stretch out the time between hair dying and even how to use a drugstore product to cover my roots when I couldn't get in for a touch-up. I went back to drugstore makeup and learned that if I had an afternoon interview, the nice women at the Nordstrom makeup counter would do my makeup for free if I just asked. (I did take them all to a nice lunch after I got a job and wrote spectacular comments in the comment cards.) I reluctantly canceled my massage subscription and became a pro at doing facials at home and went back to plucking my eyebrows myself instead of the salon waxing I was used to. I learned to keep aside enough money to get a quick manicure and "cut and color" (approximately $100) in preparation for a second interview.

I felt that investment was worth it—if I timed it right, I had work/public-appropriate hair and nails for three rounds of interviews but could also parlay it into being "the First Day of Work" ready. Sorry ladies, but life isn't fair, and this is one area where well, it just doesn't go our way. Look into having your hair done at a cosmetology school. Research a great at-home hair dye. (Go with something that is labeled semi-permanent, which will wash out, just in case.) Consider changing your hairstyle for one that is low maintenance. Do your nails at home. Look at this as temporary, and remember that you can go back to the old ways once you get back to work.

The Interview Kit is not the only unemployment hack you will need. The last thing you want is to get caught flat-footed in any area of your life. You want to be as prepared as possible for anything that comes up. I lived in fear of my car breaking down while I was unemployed or something breaking in my house. This is what you need to do is make sure you are covered.

**House Kit.** This kit makes sure you can still run your house. It is tempting to go crazy and prepare for Armageddon, but don't do that. Prepare for the quarter, the season, the next three months. Go through your home and judiciously take inventory of what you need to run your home for the next three months properly —everything from laundry detergent to toilet paper to HVAC filters. If you can do it without too much temptation, go to the store to stock up. If not, then mail-order it or order online and pick it up.

Look at your utility bills and consider paying them in advance if you can comfortably afford to do so. This is for peace of mind, but also practical reasons. You do not want to be without heat in the winter or without electricity. And in this day and age, you cannot afford to be without Wi-Fi—not when your dream job might want you to have an immediate video interview. You do not want to do that from the local Starbucks. Consider this another safety net. I don't recommend paying more than three months in advance, and I suggest contacting your utility company to tell them this is what you are doing. If the company will not allow you to do this, then put an equivalent amount aside and only use it for those bills.

**Medical Kit.** I hope you have followed my earlier advice and gone to all your doctors and your family's doctors and stocked up on prescriptions. This also includes contact lenses, by the way. Suppose it is allergy season or approaching cold and flu season, stock up on Claritin and Mucinex if you and your family go through it like water. Don't forget things such as analgesics (Advil, Tylenol, etc.). You don't have to buy the supersized bottles, but you should have a ready supply. If you take many vitamins and supplements, forgo them unless a doctor explicitly recommended them. (My doctor told me to increase my Vitamin D level and it did make a huge difference.) You will be surprised at what you really don't need and how much a healthy diet and lack of stress will improve your well-being. Go a little further and make sure you have bandages, necessary items if you have children, and sunblock if it is near summer.

Food is one of the places you will need to be very judicious. You can cut expenses and still live well. I recommend stocking up on pantry items as we have done for the pandemic—rice, pasta, jarred sauce, beans. All food that is filling and keeps well. Also, stock your freezer. Pizza as a treat, maybe a roast for celebrating getting that job or a birthday. This is one of the things I did well, and I was extremely grateful for it. I had gotten down to the wire of having no cash, and my unemployment benefits had run out. For three weeks, I lived on canned soup, pasta, beans, and rice. I even got to liven it up a little when I discovered some chicken and frozen cheese hidden in my freezer. Hello, Taco Night, thanks to the flour in my pantry and some homemade tortillas. I made it a party by inviting friends over and asking them each to bring a fixing—salsa, corn, sour cream, beer. It was one of the best dinner parties I ever threw. The idea is that, of course, you always want to have food in your house. You do not have to shop as if you will never have money again, but you will want to do all you can to assure that you and your family will have full stomachs and excellent meals.

## Additional Income

We live in a fantastic age. Even with a pandemic going on, people can still find ways to work, survive and even make some money.

Some people call it the gig economy, and some people call it the side hustle—the idea being that you do these things in addition to your regular job so that you have extra money. When you are out of work, and especially if your unemployment has run out, your side gig might become your only source of income, and it might be a godsend.

The term gig economy took off in the aughts to define the sudden influx of opportunity for people to earn extra money through nontraditional means, primarily online. Obviously, people had been earning extra income since, well, people started earning income. Some call it part-time work; some called it moonlighting — a rather romantic term meaning "my day job doesn't pay me enough." The field is more expansive than ever as internet, and cell-phone coverage increasingly blankets the country and companies such as Lyft and Instacart launch IPOs. So much so that now the pendulum has swung back, and what we know as the side hustle or gig job, is now just often referred to as work once again. The main difference is that you can now gain extra income through relatively passive means too.

**Part-Time Work.** In some ways, part-time work is the hardest means to accomplish additional income because it takes our greatest commodity—our time. There are tons of ways to get part-time work today, so many that I won't try to list them. The world is a virtual buffet to someone looking for sporadic and flexible work. Even retail outlets, crying for competent and reliable workers and competing with the online and app employer, are willing to be much more flexible about who they hire and the hours they grant. Employers used to shun highly educated and experienced individuals for fear that they would only be employed for a short time. Lately, experience and dependability override employers' concerns as they cast a larger net within the employee pool. However, there are a few things to keep in mind if you go down this road.

**Consulting.** Years ago, I had a fiancé who referred to himself as a consultant. Once a smart-alecky friend commented that "consultant" was a euphemism for "unemployed." Not anymore. Companies wishing to skirt the Affordable Healthcare Act, or taxes and benefits, look to hire contract employees with rather flexible schedules. Even websites such as LinkedIn have search features so that you can look for part-time work in your field. This is good for so many reasons. First, it allows you to stay up on trends and practices in your field, especially if it is constantly evolving, such as IT or the law. Secondly, this gives you the opportunity to network and show organizations what you could do as an employee. I have gotten at least two full-time jobs from consulting. This also allows you to see, with very little drama, if a company is a good fit for you. That goes both ways, and don't ever forget it.

Some websites allow you to control your role as a consultant in your chosen field. Sites such as Upwork and Fiverr allow you to set up a profile and negotiate your rate for your services. This is great for a side gig if you want it for extra income. I found Upwork very helpful as I tried to obtain hours to complete a certification, and I created some valuable contacts in the process. This type of job-seeking includes a substantial time investment to do it right—sometimes you need to upload a portfolio, set up a website, respond to dozens of inquiries, etc.— but it can also reap great rewards.

**Taxes and Unemployment.** You must declare your side gig income, because everything can be traced in the electronic age—or as I used to tell people in work orientations, the '*e*' in email stands for eternal. Most side hustle employers will take a fee for the work they find you. That is how they make millions and billions. Make sure you track things and make sure you know how it works before you commit your time and invest money. A friend of mine decided she wanted to drive for Lyft and spent a considerable sum bringing her car up to their standards, only to discover just how little she would make. Instacart has been in constant conflict with drivers because Instacart was not forwarding to drivers the additional tips that customers had intended for them. Also, under the pandemic conditions, some of these workers were already at risk due to the nature of their work. Additionally, the hours they were working were under additional threat as they lacked the items needed for a safe workplace such as masks and hand sanitizer. All because...

All because they were not classified as employees. Under most state laws—and this is usually a state matter—these workers are considered contract workers or part-time employees due to the hours they work and their work conditions. The rules apply to them differently. They file their taxes differently, they probably do not receive benefits, and in the cases of companies such as Lyft and Uber, these workers do not receive stock when these giants launch IPOs. There is nothing and should be nothing illegal about that, as long as all parties understand and accept this. For the typical out-of-work employee who might be used to someone else ensuring a safe work environment and receiving benefits, this can be a very sobering situation. Worker beware.

**Impact on your time and reputation.** A friend of mine worked as a Lyft driver and picked up a fare on his way into an interview. No, he did not end up driving his future boss to work, but the recruiter saw the Lyft sign in his car and him coming out of it on her way into the office. As she greeted him in the lobby, she commented upon how rough things must be for him. He felt humiliated and is convinced it impacted his interview for a director position. I hope that the COVID-19 situation changes the way we look at how others choose to live through adversity and that we look at others' job histories with a more understanding and empathetic eye (more on that later).

There is nothing wrong with one of these side gigs as long as you understand and reconcile its impact on your unemployment, reputation, and time.

## (Almost) Passive Income

Passive income provides income with little work on your part. It almost sounds too good to be true, but trust me, it is. I relied on this myself, and more than once, it saved me. In the past, people mostly earned passive income via trusts and real estate. Our current model is not much different. Real estate is still one of the main ways to generate income, but the formula has changed slightly.

**Renting Out Your Home.** Remember when you rented your first apartment on your own, and your parents probably told you to look for a two-bedroom if money got low and you needed a roommate? And you resisted because you didn't want to lose your privacy? There is now a solution to that. Airbnb, Home Away, and other such companies provide options for you to have part-time renters. I am so lucky that I live in a semi-tourist and semi-college town that has a pleasant influx of tourists for events and holidays. Before I lost my job, I used the Airbnb website to advertise my home to host guests. The extra income helped me afford a few luxuries in life, such as paying for vacations. When I lost my job, the Airbnb income became necessary for my financial survival.

If you are contemplating going this route, there are a few questions to ask yourself:

- Is the income worth having strangers stay with you?
- Do you need/want to be on property while others stay there?
- What are the "seasons" in your town?
- Do you have to lock up anything?
- What don't you want people to be allowed to do (parties, cooking, etc.) while staying in your home?
- What are the costs of renting out your home (added keys, security, amenities, etc.?

Most of the home-rental sites are extremely helpful and will walk you through the process of renting out your space. Most will even let you import the calendars of other home-rental sites so that you can manage them all at once. Many of these sites also have host forums where you can share ideas, and in some cases, rental responsibilities with other hosts in your area.

Before you open your little B&B, there are a few things to keep in mind:

**Taxes.** Taxes will differ from state to state and, in some cases, from city to city and county to county. Find out the requirements in your area. In most cases, the site will deduct the tax from your rental and pay it directly to your municipality—this covers them more than you, but it does make things very convenient for you. And you will still have to list the rental income on your taxes.

**Licensing.** This is going to vary greatly. Not every jurisdiction requires it, but some areas such as San Francisco and Santa Fe, N.M., are seeing a drought in long-term rentals because people can make more money on short-term rentals with far fewer headaches. This has resulted in strict licensing and inspections as well as annual fees to use your property for short term rental. Cities are also monitoring websites and checking to  that anyone who lists space on a short-term rental site follows the rules. I am not sure that catching the elderly couple trying to extend their Social Security by renting out their extra bedroom once or twice a month is worth that time investment—most cities I know of have bigger headaches. Sorry, it had to be said.

If you go the short-term rental route, make sure you have thought the whole thing out, from your home security to the cost of setting up your place for rental. Between startup costs (which can entail everything from locks on closet doors to extra linens) and things like hiring a cleaning service, I barely broke even in the short-term rental game. At least initially. Your mileage may vary.

**eBay.** While you have some extra time between job jobs, you should take a little time to scale down your living and storage space. Give away what you do not want or consider selling it. eBay is the ancestor of our gig economy. It is a little bit of work going in, and you do have to monitor things once they are listed and mail items once someone has won your auction. Some people and companies will list your items on eBay and even ship things for you at a cost, usually a percentage of the selling price. Think of eBay as the grownup and less time-consuming yard sale you should be having.

**Poshmark.** If you are a clotheshorse and you need extra income,

Poshmark is the site for you. Because I was only at my previous job for a short time and had shopped major sales ahead of the season, I had many clothes that I couldn't wear sitting in my closet with the tags still on them. I spent an afternoon photographing and listing my items on the Poshmark site. You have to keep an eye on this site by updating your listing and responding to offers from buyers for your items, but the reward was great. You list your clothes, and others share your listings with their followers (as a common courtesy, hoping you will share theirs with your following), and like magic, (almost) passive income arrives. This one is a bit of work as you have to mail things yourself, so you will have to obtain boxes and mail supplies. At the very least, using Poshmark helped me get rid of some extraneous gift wrap and bags I had lying around.

Some other sites purchase truly high-end merchandise from you. Usually, these items need to be exceptional and verified—think designer names such as Chanel and Hermes. Sites that offer true couture will usually have a stringent vetting process to authenticate items and figure the cost of this process into their fees.

Should you choose to sell things to generate income, keep in mind that everything is traceable. Make sure you keep meticulous records. Set aside the appropriate tax for when you submit your tax returns. Remember that even though you are out of work, you will still have to file taxes. This is not all free money.

If you choose to put one or more side hustles in action as you look for permanent work, keep track of your investment and profits. You might even opt to keep your hustle as you return to work. All decisions only you can make for You, Inc.

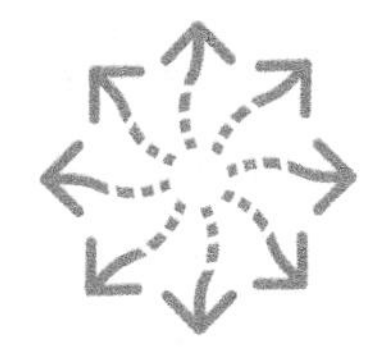

# 4

# WORKING ON GETTING BACK TO WORK

This will be a short but critical section because it addresses applying for work. Hopefully, by now, you have followed most if not all the steps to get your house in order and reflect on what you want to do. You have taken a little time for yourself. Although these steps are vital as you journey through unemployment, I hope and suggest you go through them with some speed because unless you truly apply for work, there is very little chance you will get a new job. At the same time, applying for a job is a pretty finite function. There is a limit to the amount of time you can spend each day emailing resumes, responding to posts, or even pounding the pavement (you can still get some jobs this way). The suggestions here are few, but they are important.

## Update Your Resume

Resumes are a very delicate subject. If you are seeking a job, it is very easy to identify with and become attached to your resume. For most of us, it is what got us our last appointment. I was understandably attached to the version that got me my Dream Job, convinced that if it worked once before, it would work again. My early job hunt gave all indications that I had a winner. I had a couple of quick and easy wins. I received interest on the online job boards and snared some interviews at some very prestigious organizations in the area. This just proved to me that my resume was gold. I was very proud of it and proud that I had managed to cram two solid decades of very diverse work history onto both sides of a single page.

I could not have been more wrong. Despite my early wins, by spring, I was still without a job. As most people do, when whatever I was doing isn't seeming to work, I just continued to do it harder and more. I sent my resume for anything that looked remotely close to a position I wanted. It was only after a very rough bout of walking pneumonia and a trip to visit a friend that I came out of my cocoon. I realized the aphorism was right—if you want a different result, you have to try a different action. When I realized my old resume wasn't cutting it, I decided to hire a professional resume writer. I wasted over six months before changing strategies.

I have a lot of suggestions in this book, most of which I hope you will find helpful. If you are looking for work and you only follow one of my suggestions, I hope, no I insist, that you follow this one: *Hire a professional resume writing company.*

I fought on this one. I was stubborn because I felt that no one knew me as well as I knew myself. And I am right. However, I could no longer hide from the awful truth that my phone and email were not burning up. Both were stone cold. It felt as if all recruiters in the area had put me on a list (which, of course, was not true). Giving even a small amount of money to a company to do anything, let alone something you could probably do yourself, seems like a waste of a precious resource when you are down to your last few dollars. I had that argument in my head every time I thought about hiring a resume company. I repeated it to myself after I met with a resume writing company. I continued to have that internal argument after I paid them what was, in reality, a modest amount of money to write my new resume. But at the time, it was all the money I had. Truthfully it was the last remaining amount of credit on my American Express card, an emergency resource I was holding for an emergency. Eight months without a job qualifies as an emergency. It was still a painful decision. But without a doubt, one of the best decisions I made while out of work. I couldn't argue with the results.

It was a Game-Changer! Here is how it usually works.

With great hesitation, I contacted a few resume-writing companies I found online. I set up appointments and finally chose the one I liked with fantastic testimonials and that gave me a money-back guarantee. I was instructed to look for a few jobs I found attractive that met most of my "ideal job" criteria and forward the job descriptions to the resume-writing company. I was also asked to send them my current resume and a copy of any performance evaluations or accolades I had received from recent employers.

The second meeting for my resume build was with the person who would write my resume and came only after putting down a deposit with the company. I cannot exaggerate how scary and painful that was to do. I used the very last bit of credit I had left on an American Express card. This was my last bit of "money" and was earmarked for things like food, a utility bill, or for cash in the event of an extreme emergency (I would use it for cash despite the exorbitant interest rate). Instead, I decided to take a chance on myself.

In the consultation, the resume writer and I talked about the kind of roles I was looking for, my salary requirements, the title I was seeking, the types of companies where I wanted to work, the benefits I wanted, and my employment background. *Side note—this is where having completed your mission and vision statements earlier in the book will pay off.*

The resume writer walked me through the rest of the process. She would take two weeks to write my resume. I would look at a rough draft and make suggestions, and then the company would release the final draft to me in a PDF and Word document form. They also provided a scannable version. Concerned about timing, I opted to use a little more money to have them expedite my resume for a four-day turnaround. Then I waited.

When the draft of my resume came through, I was less than pleased. I hated some of the things they put on my new resume. I was applying to executive-level roles. Why on earth did they put what software applications I knew? It would be a given that at a director level, I knew how to use Microsoft Office Suite. And I hated the formatting and how they described me, and the objective statement they wrote for me. I did not hesitate to call the company back and demand to speak to the owner. I was furious. I felt I had wasted my last few dollars.

The next day I had a passionate but productive call with the owner of the company. She did her best to talk me into using the resume (with a few tweaks) and promised that if I didn't get the results I wanted, she would personally re-do my resume or issue me a full refund. Slightly mollified, I sent the resume to a few friends, some of whom were recruiters, for feedback. *Everyone loved it.* I realized I was too emotionally close to this and agreed to give it a try. When I called back the company to give the green light to proceed, she said one of the most profound and meaningful things anyone had said to me during my job search. It is etched in my memory: **"We are not writing resumes for people, we are writing resumes for technology."**

Finally, it all made sense to me why I was not getting anywhere with my old resume. The owner of the company I used had explained to me what I will share with you.

Maybe this is obvious to you, but it wasn't to me, and my goal in this book is to help you through this journey. To help you get out of The Hole, this is crucial.

Because recruiting is automated on sites such as Indeed and LinkedIn, recruiters receive more and more resumes for fewer and fewer jobs. Last year the average number of people who applied for an open position was over a hundred. No recruiter has time to sift through that many resumes. They rely on the filters of the job sites and applicant tracking systems to do that for them. That means recruiters and companies must supply the filters with keywords, such as must-have skills, to use in sorting resumes for their company and for each position. This way, only those resumes of the truly qualified make it to the recruiter's inbox pile. The resumes might be sifted again either virtually through another set of filters or by someone who works in the recruiting office. Finally, the recruiter or hiring manager takes the last remaining resumes and chooses the lucky few to be screened and interviewed.

This was why my new resume listed the software I could use.

It should be a given that most people working in offices know how to use Google Docs and Microsoft Office Suite. Someone with multiple years under their belt might not put that on a resume in the interest of saving space, but that very omission might kick that person into the "no" pile, even if they are qualified for the job. I thought back to when I was hiring at a prior role. My main parameter for an admin was to hire someone who knew how to use our Talent Management Suite. It was like looking for a needle in a haystack. We were reduced to searching on LinkedIn for one word —the name of our system. Now it all made sense. The resume company I had hired used the job descriptions I sent them to pull the keywords from the types of jobs I was seeking to get my resume past the virtual "gatekeeper" filters and to get me into recruiters' inboxes. And this is why I urge you to leave it to the professionals, especially if your current resume, like mine, is not working. Even if you are qualified for a job, the recruiter will not know to call you if they do not see your resume, even if they are the best recruiter in the world.

I want your resume to get into the recruiter's inboxes. I cannot guarantee you that by using a service, your resume will get to the top of the pile. I cannot guarantee you will get a job. But for me, the change was like flipping a light switch. I went from the car being parked in the garage to taking it out on the Autobahn. At least, that was what it felt like. Immediately after I used the new resume, I had phone calls and emails every day from recruiters wanting to talk with me about jobs. One of those quick and immediate calls helped me land the job I ultimately accepted. I still recall meeting with one of the leaders of the company where I eventually sign on. He kept looking at my resume (the one I originally hated), telling me that it was one of the best resumes he had ever seen. Had I not changed my resume and used a service, and relied upon the power of the algorithm, this would not have happened. At least it wouldn't have happened so quickly.

## Work Your Network

Job boards and platforms are not the only way to get employed. It is a harsh reality that eighty percent of all jobs never get posted. How, you may wonder, do these roles get filled? One of the best ways to get a job is by knowing someone who works at a company who is hiring. This is one of the reasons I am so adamant that you build your network. Former colleagues, friends from high school, people from your alma mater, friends, and friends of friends can all help you get hired. But you have to ask. This can be pretty labor- and time-intensive, but it can also work.

The best approach is a direct approach. Let friends and former colleagues know you are looking for work. Our world is a much smaller place than it used to be. Send friends and former colleagues your resume. Ask if they are hiring for a role that you would be a fit for in their organization or if they know anyone who is hiring. Ask them to forward your resume to HR, just in case.

I used this technique to successfully land an interview with a global company. I had worked for this company before and left when my government contract ended. I saw a listing I thought I'd be perfect for and applied through proper channels. Then I decided not to leave anything to chance, and I looked around to see who still worked there and might remember me. Cautiously I reached out to someone in HR. I sent her a quick note mentioning when I had worked there:

*Hello, Martha (name changed at person's request),*

*I am not sure you remember me, but we met a few times when I worked for the organization from 20XX-20XX. I worked in a D.C. location on the X contract.*

*I am reaching out to you because I am looking for work and saw a job on the company website for which I'd be perfect. It matches my recent global learning and development experience along with my extensive experience in Situational Leadership, which I led for two years in my prior role. I would appreciate it if you could forward my resume to HR, and I am happy to have a quick call with you to discuss.*

*Sincerely,*

*Sabina*

*P.S.— I am wondering, did you ever get to meet the First Lady?*

My note reminded her that we did not directly work together but that we had met. I also made sure she could look up the contract on which I worked. I wanted her to be sure I was qualified for the job and that she could forward my resume with confidence. I also added the note about the former First Lady so she could be sure that we had in fact met. Meeting Michelle Obama was high on her Bucket List.

Much to my surprise, Martha wrote back to me that she did indeed remember me and that she had forwarded my resume to HR and had recommended me for the job. This was beyond my expectations. Sometimes you have to go through a different path to get you where you want to be. I wrote back to thank Martha and to sheepishly acknowledge that she had gone above and beyond as I had not exactly been in touch with her for a while. I believe her response says it all: *No problem, Sabina, It's called making the Network work!*

Make your network work for you and then, of course, always return the favor.

## Use Recruiting Firms and Staffing Agencies with Caution

A quick note about recruiting firms: it is very flattering if one of them calls you up out of the blue. Usually, they will have gotten your name from a friend, or they have searched for someone with your talents on LinkedIn, or you have put a flag on your profile that you are open to opportunities.

Executive recruiting firms can be beneficial and very seductive. They are valuable because they come to you and they do all the hard work. They have usually built up a relationship with the hiring company, and it can often be like a velvet rope has been lifted that gets you inside the club to the VIP Interview section with minimal effort on your part. Recruiting firms usually prep you thoroughly for a role. All of this can be glamorous and exciting, especially if you have been unemployed for a while. And if this works out for you, it is amazing. You get a wonderful job— most firms are very picky and only handle high-level positions—and they earn a living. And you now have a go-to for life because you were a successful candidate for them, and therefore, you have an excellent track record as far as they are concerned. I have seen search firms keep successful candidates on file and return to them when other, often juicier, roles come to the firm's attention.

Here are a few things to keep in mind: you will hear this from me repeatedly: *Invest but do not attach.* My own experience with these firms has been positive and eye-opening. I was once a very hot commodity with one of these firms. A friend had recommended the company to me, and I was very impressed by the CEO, a well-spoken and polished individual who was also very empathetic. I appreciated that he was honest and told me he had nothing to offer me at the time. He seldom had job opportunities available in my line of work, but that he would keep me in mind. I was more than a little surprised when he called me almost a year later with an opportunity. I was a bit naive in the process. The job sounded too good to be true: a great salary and a good company. I was a little concerned because no one would tell me why the position was open. The prior head of learning had only been in the job for a few months, and I was told it just didn't work out. I went to the interview and immediately clicked with the head of HR. It went so well that the search firm called me before I got home to set up the next round of interviews, which would be a full day of interviewing with the team. I went in a week later and felt exceptionally good about things. It went so well that as I was leaving the second round of interviews, the head of HR asked if I could start within the week. The rep at the search firm was incredibly enthusiastic. He told me he would call me by the end of the following week.

By that Friday, I had received no call. By the following Monday, I knew I didn't get it. Finally, on Tuesday, the head of the search firm called to tell me that the company's CEO had reservations that I had held too many jobs in too short a time for his liking. Let me say something about that. All of the roles I took were progressive that offered more responsibility and let me focus on a different part of my field. They all offered more money and better benefits. I cannot help but feel the CEO was out of touch on this point. But the harder lesson for me to learn was that I was nothing more than a commodity to the search firm, which I thought was grooming me and was in my corner. What I hadn't realized was that they had other candidates up for the role, and who got the position did not matter to them. What they cared about was that they provided the person who ultimately got the position. It was a hard lesson for me to digest. These people were not my buddy or pal. They were not working for me. I was just a piece of inventory to them. I am not saying this firm did anything wrong. I am saying *I* did not have a complete understanding of the situation. It would have been wonderful if they had taken up my case with the CEO, but they had no incentive to do so as long as he was more than happy to take on another one of their candidates for the role. I attached when I should have invested. Do not let this happen to you. Not all search firms operate this way, but most of them do. By all means, explore all possibilities but do not invest more effort or energy than you have to. Have a very open and honest conversation with the firm about their process and whether or not they are forwarding candidates other than yourself for a role. Do not misconstrue friendliness for investment or friendship. Do not be seduced by a bright shiny object.

As you can see, you have multiple options available to you as you pursue a job and a career. I want the majority of your investment to be into learning what you want and need to be, combined with a viable strategy for exploring and using your options to the fullest. Once you know your path and have a firm resume, sending it out and even looking at the job market daily will not take the majority of your time. It will, of course, be the most precious effort and actions you take in the job search. You want to be optimally prepared and focused.

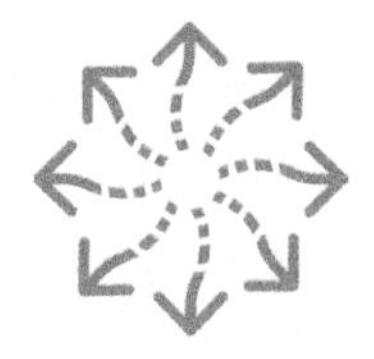

# 5
# THE IMPORTANCE OF NETWORKING

By now, you have done a few things so that you are ready to begin to look for work. Mind you; there is no specific order for this. Although looking for work is a full-time job, it will eventually be something in a maintenance phase. You will have done all of your pre-work—finances, health, home, reflection, and resume—and you are ready to start. Although a few of the tasks I recommend are time-sensitive, none of the tasks I am suggesting you complete need to be done in a specific order. Your doing them will overlap one another. You will probably be sending out resumes as you are getting your budget together. As you get your home in order, you should be reflecting upon what you want to do with your life as you write and hone your mission and vision statements. There is very little right or wrong here, except for the things I have mentioned that are time-bound and, of course, looking for work. As I said earlier, you are eleven to twenty-two weeks away from finding a new job -- every second counts.

The following suggestions are crucial, even if you have not settled on what you need or want the next phase of your career to be. If you are still reflecting and trying to figure out what you want to change career paths, some of these suggestions will help you make that change a reality.

## Networking

Let's get the most challenging part of this out in the open. Not everyone is a social butterfly. I am not. Meeting new people has always been difficult for me. I am extremely shy and very uneasy in situations where I don't know anyone. In writing this section of the book, I reached out to a friend, Andy Storch, self-described Talent Connector and author of *Own Your Career Own Your Life*. Andy makes networking look easy. He effortlessly reaches out to people to build his own network and to build a learning community. As I was writing this book, I asked Andy for advice to give people like myself who struggle with reaching out to others. He stressed above everything else that if you are sincere in how you reach out to others, you have a great chance of making an actual connection. People will see your sincerity, putting them in the frame of mind to respond positively to your request. This ties right back to the mission and vision statements I had you write earlier. You can use them as the framework of your "ask." Knowing why you are reaching out to certain people will increase your confidence and help you make positive and helpful connections as you pursue a job and as your career evolves.

Another point Andy stresses is that it is all right if someone says "no." We never know what someone else is going through and what they have on their plate. It is natural in this process to receive a "no" every now and then, and we have to be OK with that. It is not necessarily a reflection of us. "No" could mean "not now." We have to understand and respect the other person's choice not to connect and to move on.

Today's virtual world has granted us many advantages and gifts. We can reach more people more quickly. But does that grant us closeness and intimacy or even connection? Keep in mind that the way you connect with an individual and continue that connection directly reflects the relationship itself. A few years ago, a commercial showed a young woman talking about all her friends online. The total was in the thousands. She took this as a sign of her popularity. She bemoaned that her parents, on the other hand, had only seven friends online. She thought that was lame. Her parents then spoke to the camera about all the trips they were taking and the richness of their relationships. I think in this day and age, we land somewhere in between. We make friends online and in-person for various reasons. The network you forge should reflect the state of your world at the moment. You get into it what you put into it, as the saying goes. A network may be regarded as something you have, but I believe that a network is something you need, even if you do not need all parts of it all the time. It is much like a garden. Your network consists of living beings. You tend to each section of your garden as you need it—vegetables in the summer, flowers in the spring, herbs as needed, perennials all the time. Your network should be run much the same way, but keep in mind that you should always tend to your network and not look at it as a collection you keep closed off in a curio cabinet to symbolize your popularity.

Your network should reflect you as a complete person, not just one part of you. For example, it shouldn't just reflect your hobbies, family, or school chums from days gone by, but all of the above, for a host of reasons. First and foremost, you are a holistic human being. We are in better health the more well-rounded we are. Work will probably be the biggest time ask of your life, but it should not wholly define you.

This is never more apparent when you lose a job. What you once used as your identifier is gone, leaving you with a complete lack of base and identity. Having the soft cushion of family and hobbies and friendships to busy us is essential. Even if you made the error of solely focusing on your work network, you could always build your network—and now is the time.

Networks are living organisms, mainly because they are formed of and by of living creatures, however they survive and thrive in two different ways. One of the most obvious is how we build the network around ourselves. In the insect world, queen ants and queen bees are the centers of their insect universes. All other beings in the hive or colony work for the queen, and thus, for the colony or hive itself. Those insect worlds thrive around the queen because the queen is the life source—she is the one who lays the eggs and allows new life into the colony. If the queen stops producing eggs, the colony dies, even if all other members continue to do their jobs. If each colony member fails to do its part, no matter how much the queen produces new life, the colony dies. You are the center or life force of your network. You give it definition and life. You are solely responsible for its health and wellbeing—even if everyone else continues to do their part. By the same token, you need that group to keep your life going. When you ask others to join your network, you are also, in essence, joining theirs. It is so easy to say "yes" to anyone who wants to join your network as you are trying to build a professional identity. However, be selective and strategic. Consider: is adding this person going to help your network thrive *and* can you be an active and contributing member to theirs? Would you rather have a smaller, stronger, relevant and well-rounded network, or a large, extended one? Only you can make that decision for yourself.

Let's take a moment and talk about methodology—how you connect with others. I often work with students from my alma mater as they begin their careers. Resumes, interviews, and networking are vital topics for students. In every workshop, one caution is to demand that students look at their digital footprint by doing an internet search on themselves. Sometimes they are more than a little shocked at what they find. People "tag" their friends on social media, and that information spreads to friends of friends. You never know where you are going to show up, and the larger your network, the larger the possibility of showing up somewhere you don't want to be "seen." People who tag others seldom check first. It is a given that if you post something online or a friend of yours does, specifically a photo, it will be found. Social media such as Facebook, Instagram, TikTok, etc., can render all of our lives public fodder. Even LinkedIn, once the refuge of respectability, is not immune.

Photos aren't the only thing that lives forever online. If you comment on something online, even if it is a local paper or an industry forum, there is a permanent record of it. Every once in a while, I see someone make a questionable comment on LinkedIn, and just shake my head, wondering whether the commenter understands that others are reading their opinions. Sometimes, it is not what they say, but how they say it. Improper language, poor grammar or spelling, and derogatory posts are never the mark of a professional.

This is all-important as you network because the company you keep is a reflection of you. And prospective employers will be looking. This can work in your favor as well as against you, so let's make it work for you. I suggest you do a search on yourself to see what comes up. Make sure that if there is something questionable, you can at least explain it if it comes up in an interview, even if you cannot correct it. I once interviewed someone to be chief legal counsel for a nonprofit where I volunteered. We did a quick internet search and found several mugshots of the individual. This obviously had us on guard, but his resume was flawless, as were his references and reputation in the field. We were so concerned that we asked to interview him at a local coffeehouse initially. He arrived early (a good sign) and sailed through the interview with flying colors. We were disarmed and charmed. As a closing question, we asked if they had anything he wanted to ask us or that he wanted us to know about him. Luckily, he was very savvy and could read people and situations. He asked if we had Googled him and if that was why we asked to meet in public. We answered affirmatively. He voluntarily told us the reason for the arrest was because he had been part of a peaceful demonstration protesting lack of safety processes at a factory in his local state (a family member worked there). He had been arrested with a dozen other people. All charges had been dropped. We hired him a week later.

As you build your network, do so mindfully, intelligently, and strategically. Even when you are employed, to develop your professional network, I would stick to sites like LinkedIn or other professional forums. I would avoid social media that tends to be too personal, such as Facebook, Instagram, etc. In the early days of social media, I reported to a manager who intensely pressured everyone she supervised to join her page on a particular platform. I resisted, and she once used it as a reason not to put me on a project, stating I was aloof and using the example of my refusal to join the platform as proof. A few months later, our head of HR had some potentially embarrassing photos of herself show up on social media. She had innocently gone on a weekend in Vegas with some friends from college and posted the pictures. Nothing too audacious, but you just don't want to see one of your bosses living it up in Sin City. Although she had posted pictures of her vacation privately, some coworkers who were part of her online network tagged her in their public posts. What happens in Vegas does not always stay in Vegas. Shortly after that, the company posted a social media policy against tagging fellow employees without permission. Lesson learned.

## Platforms

**LinkedIn.** LinkedIn is the chameleon of social media. It started as a networking place for professionals to meet and quickly morphed into a job board. Most of LinkedIn's revenue now comes from selling access to its members' information to organizations and recruiters. More recently, LinkedIn has become a learning resource and a social media platform where members post their thoughts, ideas, and projects. Membership on LinkedIn is free unless you elect to upgrade your membership level to receive permissions such as searching on the platform incognito. The site allows members to search using select filters, which makes it an ideal networking tool. All members are identified by a degree of separation identifier—"1st" meaning you have connected directly with the person on the platform, "2nd" meaning you are connected to someone who knows them, etc. Other filters let you search for members who work for a particular company or who went to a specific school.

When we think of reaching out and networking, our world is such that we tend to think of doing this online—especially in the world of COVID. Although LinkedIn is a tried-and-true way to network and search for jobs, it is by no means the only way. Other platforms are slowly but surely being used by people who want to broaden their professional circle.

**Meetup.com.** No longer just a site for weekend athletes and foodies. Meetup has started to generate professional working groups. Meetup is a rarity in that groups and activities planned on the platform are created for the main purpose of meeting in person, usually in a larger city or geographical region.

**MyOpportunity.com.** Opportunity's whole purpose is to help professionals generate leads and networks. It is picking up in popularity.

**Jobcase.com.** Although its main purpose seems to be finding job leads, it does have a community section and looks to increase this offering.

**Lunchclub**. Lunchclub is an online meeting space. Participants fill out a brief questionnaire, and the platform matches you based upon your answers. Users get weekly reminders to sign up for meetings and control how many forty-five-minute sessions a week they schedule. The platform matches users based upon their interests and their profession. After each call, participants can rate the call and identify whether it was a good match for them and their professional needs. It can take a few meetings before your matches genuinely meet your needs. Participants can also earn points by inviting members of their own networks to join the Lunchclub site. Once they have reached a certain level of participation, users are invited to join partner sites of the platform for executives and other groups.

You want to cast as large a net as possible, especially if you are looking for work. Besides websites that offer networking, there are apps (I would be careful with this) such as LunchMeet that allow professionals in the same area to meet one-on-one and social media such as Twitter mention local sites and events for networking. This can come in handy for building your professional circle. Now that we have discussed where to do it, let's discuss how to build your network.

## Building Your Network

I went to a very small, specialized college in Maryland. Through an odd set of circumstances, I ended up being elected to our Alumni Board. We were tasked with helping to improve the engagement of our alumni community. Before I joined the board, a consultant had come to the campus to determine why alumni were so passionate about the school but wanted little to do with the school after they graduated. They were happy to interact with other alums, just not by using the school as the vehicle to do so. As a board and in partnership with the college, we looked at ways we could build our relationship with future alumni by supporting our current students. We developed strategies to help them find internships and summer employment. We taught them to network and how to look for employment before graduation.

We sought to help them build their alumni networks as students and taught them how to use them professionally. We are now looking for ways to support alumni through career changes and offer college resources to help them build career skills and connect to other professionals in their field. We actively seek panelists to help all community members learn about new career paths and strengthen existing ones. *The key to all of this is showing our value to our audience rather than making it about us.* We have answered the seldom-asked but often-thought question, **What is in it for them?** You need to answer as you are building your network—not why do you want that person in your network, but why should they join your team? If you can successfully answer that, then you will build a healthy and thriving network.

## Connect with Colleagues

It is always good to connect with people you work with, but be careful about it. I suggest connecting with peers at work. This shows an interest in them and allows you to learn about them. In some workplaces, this is part of the culture. In others, it is almost forbidden. The best way to learn how your workplace functions is to wait until a few people have connected with you. There seems to exist a trend of meeting someone new at work and then, if the culture allows a day or two later, they invite you to connect, usually on LinkedIn. This opens the door for you to do the same. I would suggest keeping this on LinkedIn as opposed to Facebook or a strictly social form of networking. You want to keep your personal world and your private one from overlapping too much. Once you open that door to the person, it is very hard to close it, if not impossible.

When building your work network, don't just connect with everyone in your office. It's a good idea to meet people from other areas of your organization so you can build a network of people whose work expertise you value that is a mixture of peers and potential mentors. I would not suggest trying to connect to your company's CEO—chances are they have a closed network for a reason. The head of your functional area? Maybe, but only if you have met them personally or have an "in," such as having attended a talk they gave or working together on a committee. Have the decency not to barrage them with requests. If you put out the request once and they do not respond, let it go. Be OK with the "No."

## Connect with Colleagues in Your Line of Work

Another way to build your work network is to reach out to peers outside your company—people who hold a similar job title to yours in other organizations and industries. Hint: You will be likelier to do this if you contact them with a reason and some knowledge of their organization. For example, when I worked for an organization in downtown D.C., I wanted to start an informal gathering of local learning professionals. I wanted us to meet quarterly to discuss best practices, challenges we all faced, etc. Peers at my workplace told me that people from other organizations would refuse to meet with me. Undaunted, I sent out connection requests. Because I had sent out careful parameters, almost every request I made was answered. My ask was so small that the main response I received was along the lines of *I don't have time to pull anything formal together, but if you want to meet for coffee one morning, I can do that.* From there, several coffees later, I was able to pull together one well-attended breakfast of about twenty learning professionals from the area. Although I left my job shortly after that initial breakfast, I understand that the group still gathers informally. Most of them had never met each other until that first breakfast, and all of us are a part of each other's networks.

It never hurts to build a network of those who do what you do; this should be the core of your work network. Your network should be a reflection of you professionally—where you have been and where you want to go, not just a reflection of the places where you have worked. In building your network, do not be seduced by adding only those you believe are in a position of power to help you. Instead, build your network of people whose work you genuinely admire. Networks are like friendships and initially like gathers like—most likely, your network is a group of people much like yourself who do the same thing at the same level. Consider surrounding yourself with people who have a skill set or opinion the opposite of yours and people who will make you work just a little bit harder. Andy Storch stresses that one of the best reasons to reach out to someone is to learn from them. Consider the difference between sending someone an email or a request on LinkedIn that is just a connection request, versus the same email or connection request that has a brief note stating, *"I saw on a recent LinkedIn post of yours that you helped your company develop a Manage from Home toolkit. I have recently been assigned to lead a team scattered across the country, and I would love to learn more about the work you've done."* You have asked someone to teach you, and few people can say "no" to that. People love to help others and talk about themselves and their work. You may never need these people to help you get a job, but that should never, ever be the point of your network anyway. Your network should be an entity of support and buoyancy to help you hone and sharpen and elevate your skills, to help you identify new ones, to make you a better person or practitioner—to teach you.

You can pull the work section of your network together by profession or industry, or both as I did. Keep in mind you need to tend to this part of your network often. You need to make an effort to reach out to these members, if not to meet with them in real life. Luckily again, social media makes this very easy for us. One easy and effortless way to do this is to share an article or podcast online. At least once a week, I reach out to my network, suggesting a podcast to them with intelligent reasoning. If they are managers, I reach out with a new book I read that tells them a great coaching model, or I give them a site to follow. *The idea is that you tend to your work network and are an active member of it.* The hope is that if you need someone from your network, they will be more likely to help you because you have attempted to help them.

You were not just the person they have nothing in common with who reached out to them solely because you were looking for a job interview or to increase the size of your network. They will recommend you and share your name because you have reached out to them in good faith and with purpose.

## Education Connections

One of the wonderful things about age and time is that they are great equalizers, but the thing we still have in common with the people we went to school with is just that—the institutions themselves. No matter who or what you were in school, there is something about a shared alma mater that pulls people together. When I was in college, I recall being at O'Hare airport coming back from visiting a friend during a break. There, waiting at the gate was someone I knew from school with whom I had never spoken. Although it was a small school we did not travel in the same social circle. We did that distant familiarity nod at the gate as we waited for our flight and ran into each other again at one of the snack bars. I was short on funds and did not have enough cash to cover my pretzel and soda. Sure enough, an unfamiliar voice offered to make up for my lack of funds: This fellow student covered my snack. We didn't talk on the plane as we were on separate rows, but upon arrival in Baltimore, he offered to share his ride back to campus with me, rightly guessing that I did not have cab fare. Later, back on campus, I repaid his money with a nice note, but we never spoke after that. Not because we didn't get along, but we were not close friends. I learned something from the experience: Even people who are not your friend will have your back when you need them if you have something in common, especially if you have a shared experience.

Do not discount the common alliance you have with people from your alma mater. I have avidly reached out to people from high school, college, grad school, certification courses and asked them for help. Rarely am I refused, even if years have gone by or we never crossed paths in the first place. The common connection is connection enough. You always want to help someone who went through a similar experience. I urge you to look for people you might know on any platform who might be able to introduce you to a recruiter, someone in HR, a hiring manager, someone in the field in which you practice, or someone in a field in which you are interested. That is what these connections are for—to help each other. And one day, I am sure someone from your alma mater will reach out to you for the same reason.

## Find a Mentor

I cannot stress enough the importance of having mentors while on the job and out of work. The role of a mentor is to help you grow and develop, be a coach and a sounding board, and to hold you accountable. I have been lucky in my career to have had several mentors and to be a mentor myself. Few things are as satisfying as helping someone succeed in the workplace. To be beneficial to both parties, the mentor/mentee relationship must be held seriously and sacrosanct to by all. Mentors help mentees grow professionally buy also take on a protective role to advise and help their mentee. They remove obstacles and roadblocks, and they challenge and support.

Several jobs ago, I had a colleague who scared me to no end. He was a tall, imposing man and highly demanding. He was an amazing leader—when he asked you to do something, you did it as if you were being asked to find the Holy Grail. No matter how important or how menial the task, you felt as if you were special by being singled out to do it. People lined up to be in his circle. He was one of the few people in my career I felt had a natural charisma and leadership instinct. At the same time and in the same workplace, I got to work with another colleague. She was cut of a different cloth but just as impressive and imposing. Where he ruled with an iron fist, she ruled with a firm and soften voice. He was brusque and to the point. She was more collaborative, but equally direct. Both were high ranking within the company, and both had amazing career achievements. His claim to fame was having been a manager at Heathrow airport during 9/11. Hers was to have been the youngest project manager in the history of a certain Fortune 100 company.

It was the easiest and hardest stint in my career. Easy because both were some of the few leaders I have ever worked with who understood the necessity of learning, development, and talent management—which made my job both easier and harder. Easier because it was one of the few times I had leaders who understood and supported what I could do for an organization, and hard because both of them had set high standards and expectations for me and my work. They had opposite ways of working with me and asking things of me—he barked orders but trusted me to plan the strategy and execute it. She was more collaborative and communicative. He, oddly enough, was much more understanding of a missed deadline or failure to execute. She, on the other hand, was not. I will never forget when she and I passed each other in the ladies' room, and she quietly asked me about a deliverable. I stated that I was unclear about the due date. Her response was, *I expected you to do it when I asked.* Yes, ma'am. I never let her down again. When I missed a certain expectation of his, he reacted by taking me to the bar across from the office and buying me a drink. He spoke of his childhood and family and how important trust was to him. He ended by stating that he trusted me and more importantly he trusted that I would never let him down again. I never did. I neither loved them both nor feared them both. To paraphrase Michael Scott of *The Office*—I feared how much I loved them, and some days, I loved how much I feared them. Both made me work hard. Both made me increase my skillset and stretch myself. Both made it clear they were not asking anything of me that I could not do, and both made it a point to guide and protect my career. Once, I had been working to set up an internal website for our U.S. employees, but all the information I needed was being held by another department, in another country. I spent weeks reaching out to the head of the department, whom I knew. He came up with dozens of excuses as to why he had been unable to get me the information—things like it was in the wrong format for my technology, it was proprietary, etc. I mentioned this to my mentor during a one-on-one. One day as if by magic, I received an email from the head of the department with all the files attached and an offer to set up a meeting to walk me through all the material. I was able to set up the website in a week, and when I did, my mentor made sure to send a note to my manager stating that I had knocked it out of the park as usual. When I asked him in person months later whether he had been the one to open the door for me, he shrugged and just said, "Maybe." I appreciated that he had stood back to allow me to try every possible avenue to make this website happen and then intervened when he realized I had hit an obstacle I couldn't cross. From then on, whenever I needed information from that group, I had this man's clout behind me and was never refused. We need more mentors in this world.

# Find a Younger Mentor

Too often, we link the benefits of a mentor's connections and experience to the time they have put into something, rather than their actual skill set. A crucial life lesson came to me when helping students at my college prepare for job interviews. I met a lovely young woman from Korea who was concerned about her English skills. We worked for hours to hone her interview and speaking skills, only to discover that the issue was not her grasp of the English language, which was probably better than my own, but rather a lack of confidence in speaking a second language. One of the ways we chose to work on that was to have her teach me something, figuring that if I could grasp what she was telling me enough to learn from it, then her skill level in the language was high. As chance would have it, she was very knowledgeable in the presentation application Prezi. I wanted to learn more about it and very much wanted to revamp my resume by having someone (or myself) put my resume in Prezi form to update and refresh it. She offered to do so, but instead, we decided to test her English skills by having her teach me to do it. She was a much better teacher than I was a student, but I discovered that she was extremely savvy in social media through this endeavor. We added this to her resume and positioned her as a social media expert for me and others in the college community.

As fate would have it, she ended up taking a job in her native South Korea in social media. I still reach out to her from time to time with questions and am always flattered that she makes time for me. This relationship showed me, among other things, that my mentors do not always have to be my age or older. I learned far more from someone younger than myself because your mentor does not necessarily have to have life experience. One of the criteria you set should be that they are more skilled than you are in something you wish to achieve.

We now have four or five generations in the workplace, and you will probably find yourself in the position of working with peers and bosses who are younger than you are. This can be a challenge for anyone. One way to clear this hurdle is to realize that allowing yourself to be mentored by someone younger shows you are adapting to the fact that you can learn from anyone. And you should learn from everyone. It's how you will adjust to the changes we are experiencing in the workplace.

## Become a Mentor Yourself

One of the best ways to get through a difficult time is to remember how lucky you are and to share your gifts with others. There will always be someone better off than you are and worse off than you are. You will be happier if you learn from both groups. I found that mentoring others while searching for a job often took me outside myself and my feelings of depression and anxiety. At my alma mater, I annually serve on a panel to help students write their resumes and to help prepare them for the job market. It was fortuitous that the date for the annual panel fell right after I lost my job. I was able to work with multiple students and help them prepare for all aspects of interviews, including resumes, interviews, proper attire, and business etiquette. This group of students helped me far more than I helped them. The workshop gave me a tremendous feeling of being needed and appreciated.

As I went through the job hunt, one recruiter commented that they brought me in to interview despite my age (thank you) because I had so many connections in the Millennial and Gen Z category on LinkedIn. It also didn't hurt that I had a couple of testimonials from students about how well I understood their situation and how much I helped them in their job search.

I have found that it is easier to find a mentor than it is to become one. My suggestion is to look within your community—a house of worship, an after-school program, a college, a professional forum, etc. On a site such as LinkedIn, you can respectfully say that you are looking for an opportunity to mentor someone, especially if you have vast experience in a field. It can become one of the most rewarding relationships in your career.

To summarize, here is a list of the people you should have in your network. Keep in mind your network is a living entity that reflects you and your career and that different parts of your network will thrive at different times in your career. I am asking you to rethink work. You will not just use this network to look for a job, but also learn and continue to evolve. Think of your network as the unofficial advisors and consultants of You Inc.

The network of You, Inc:

- Friends (and family)
- Current or recent coworkers
- Former coworkers with whom you shared a department or job role
- People in your field from whom you can learn
- People who make you think things differently
- Mentors
- Mentees
- Fellow alumni
- People with whom you share a professional organization or interest
- People whose careers you wish to emulate

Remember that you should go through your network at least once a year to make sure it is up to date. This is especially true on sites that limit the number of contacts you can have. Think of this as you tending to your garden and keeping it thriving.

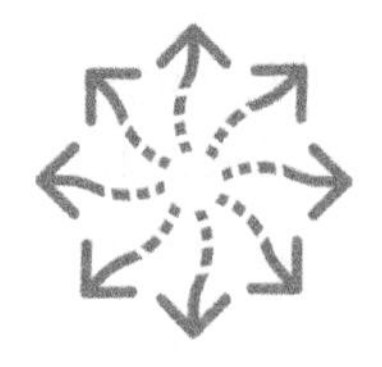

# 6
# MINDFUL EXTREME SELF-CARE

Once you have your house in order and your resume updated and going out, you will find yourself in a cycle of waking up and applying and looking for work. No matter how hard you look for work and connect with others about looking for work, you will find that this does not take up your entire day. Nor should it. Remember looking for work is now a top priority—it takes the place of your former job. However, it is not and should not be all that you do. To be a healthy human being, you will need to find other things to fill your day.

I am not saying that you should not put an incredible amount of energy and time into looking for work. I am advocating the opposite. However, it is possible to become too consumed with looking for work. I do not want that for you. I want you to look for work. I want you to find a job. But I also want you to be a well-balanced, healthy person. My last job, before I lost it, consumed my life. I worked twelve- to fourteen-hour days, including the weekend. My life was work, sleep, repeat. I stopped seeing friends and doing the things I loved to do. I knew it had gotten to an unhealthy level when I found myself taking a business call while hooked up to an iron IV.

If you allow your job search to take over your life, you run the risk of not only closing out the important things in your life, such as family and friends, but you risk your health. If possible, I want you to come out of this a healthier, more balanced person than when you lost your job. And that means finding an equilibrium between looking for work and working on yourself. There should be harmony between your job search and the rest of your life. If you over-focus on the job hunt, it can consume you and mire you in the emotions it can bring on through the roller coaster of hopefulness and disappointment. Having an equal focus on other parts of your life will help you not fall victim to the perils of the job hunt, such as anxiety and depression. If you were like me and work defined and consumed you, you have a huge gap in your life to fill.

If you aren't convinced yet, let's look at it this way. Your house is in order, you have established your career goals, and you are doing the actions needed to reach them—you are applying for jobs. All of this is what most organizations call BAU—Business As Usual. The companies that succeed and expand are the companies that go beyond BAU. They are the ones that focus on constant targeted improvement, often called "organizational health." Look at the activities you have already completed to ensure that You, Inc. is running at an optimal BAU. Now, look at what You, Inc. needs to do to improve constantly and consistently.

At the onset of this book, I told you that I wanted you to look at being unemployed in a new light. This balance is a massive part of it. I want you to develop a mindset and habits to carry through to your future job and life. I want you to also make yourself a priority. I want you to practice Mindful Extreme Self-Care and Self Development.

I am frequently asked by clients if there is a difference between Extreme Self-Care and Development. In my mind, there is no difference. You can look at self-care as things you want to do for yourself, such as exercise and getting enough sleep, and development as something you have to do, such as learning.

For me, both are tied to helping you become an empowered and well-rounded individual during your time of unemployment and beyond. If you think of yourself as You, Inc., think of how organizations run themselves. There are the things they must do to be leaders in their field, meet government mandates, and keep the doors open, such as paying taxes. If you think of yourself that way, you will realize that some things you might not enjoy, such as earning a certification, that might be a missing piece to becoming employed. Or it may be the thing that helps you stand out from your competitors. We are more apt to think of self-care as pampering and rewards. I want you to think of extreme self-care as anything necessary for your overall health and well-being that also advances your mission and vision statements. Self-care is needed for you to function fully as a person and as an employee. This is why both are essential. No matter what you choose to call it, it will be important for you to establish a routine of Self-Care or Development.

## Design a Routine

Remember how you wrote out your mission statement—what you are working on now—and your vision statement—your ideal of what you ultimately want to do/be? Your routine should encompass items that will help you achieve both. Your routine should balance your immediate needs of taking care of yourself and looking for a job as well as some of your visionary, ultimate path or dream. Just as organizations balance what they must do and want to do, your routine should reflect that. Every day organizations perform the work that helps them achieve their annual goals while also turning an eye and some energy and resources toward their future. This is what your routine would do. You must work toward any goal, or it really is just fantasy. The Alzheimer's Association runs its day-to-day business and also seeks out new research and development in the fight against the disease.

Otherwise, it would not be able to envision *A world without Alzheimer's*. The power that comes from having a routine is that it is **your** plan toward achieving your mission and vision. It is not the plan someone else sets for you; it is what you choose for yourself. Rather than being the victim of change, you flip the paradigm by the decisions you make. In the words of thought leader David Richo, "We are not changing, we are choosing." You have determined your Now and your Future, and your routine is the path and structure to get you from one to the other.

My routine was influenced by a host of things, one of which was my being prone to anxiety and depression. I found that the meditation and afternoon exercise I eventually scheduled did wonders for self-soothing and for helping me to keep emotions at bay without using medication. Reading became incredibly important to me. I had devised a list of things to do by the time the year was over, and one of them was to read one book for every year of my life. (Notice I am not giving you that number.) I had a little routine and ritual set up with reading. I wrote down the book I was reading and kept track of how long it took me to get through it. I mixed up the genres I read to make it interesting—some work-related books and some fun escapist books. This served several purposes. First, it filled up my day. Structure prevented me from doing things such as mindlessly watching TV. Instead, I began reading books that had sat on my shelf for years, collecting dust. As I completed each book, I moved it to a separate, empty shelf where I started stacking all the books I had read. I got a sense of accomplishment every time I passed that shelf. I am trying to do the same thing now, as I write this during the pandemic. I have mixed it up a little by starting a book group with friends and trying to record our book club meetings as podcasts and have members of the group write and post our book reviews. This is a way of keeping my skill set at its best and stretching myself a little.

Your routine should vary and should reflect you. Mine was a tad easier to achieve because I lived alone, and I deliberately planned every single moment. This gave me structure and prevented bad habits from creeping in. I tried to add free time and flexibility, but I found I got anxious and cranky if I had to forgo what I called Personal Development for a job interview or to meet with friends. All this carefully crafted structure fell to the wayside when I got a job, and one of my goals is to bring some of these practices to my everyday life.

Not putting myself first and focusing too much on the job search was another mistake I made while unemployed. I found myself in a terrible cycle of wake up, apply for jobs, get no response, be depressed, lie on the couch all day until it was time to sleep. Getting sick with walking pneumonia drove me further into depression. It was only when a very savvy and well-meaning friend had me visit her that I began to climb out of the metaphorical hole I had dug for myself. Maybe it resulted from being in a warm sunny climate for a change or just being around my friend's constant encouragement, but that trip gave me the jump start I needed to begin climbing out of my funk. My three days along the Gulf coast gave me the structure I had been lacking. Every moment of our time was carefully planned and scheduled. Meals, visits, even TV time were strictly structured. I just didn't realize it until the plane ride home. It was then that I understood the positive impact of putting structure in my day. I needed to start making my health and well-being a priority. This flash of insight into the need for self-care had an immediate positive impact on my life and job search. I have a million excuses as to why I did not successfully establish a routine earlier, the primary reason being that, logically, I was going to get a job soon. So who needs a routine? You do.

I built mine slowly. Early in my exile from the Land of Having a Job, I had begun to read a book called *Creating Your Best Life: The Ultimate Life List Guide* by Caroline Adams Miller, MAPP, and Dr. Michael B.

Frisch. For years this book sat on my shelf untouched. Newly unemployed, I thought this would be a good time to begin reading it and following it. I got to Chapter Three. I stopped because of all the reasons I listed before—I had gotten some interviews, I had the holidays, and finally, I just let things slip. After my trip to the Gulf, I picked the book up again, hoping that even reading one hour a day would give me structure. In addition to providing reading material, this book brought me the structure and purpose I craved. In this book, I found multiple practices to help me develop habits to defeat anxiety and depression. I found a way to vocalize how I wanted my life to be. It would take a pandemic for me to build and adopt a self-care routine that met most of my health and wellness goals. Keep in mind that you do not have to do everything while you are unemployed. Development never stops. But the habits you form now should carry over to after you return to work.

A good structure is essential for humans. A structured daily routine can be beneficial in dealing with stress and anxiety. Having a given time when certain things get done alleviates the anxiety that comes with the unknown. Following a routine causes a person to be active, even if they are just sitting, and it occupies the mind, which can quell feelings of depression and anxiety. Completing items or routines can give the individual a sense of accomplishment. It's the same sense of accomplishment we receive when we complete a project or task at work. The same sense of accomplishment we stopped receiving when we lost our jobs. Building and completing a routine fills that void.

I didn't realize it at the time but opening that book and setting aside an hour a day to go through it would ultimately become a well-thought-out routine that forced me to focus on my future and myself. My routine not only drew me out of depression, but it anchored me. It made looking for work more bearable. It made me feel proactive and accomplished despite a slow job search. A routine that focused on my specific needs began to make me feel whole and human. It gave me a purpose to get up every morning. I confess that prior to setting up a structure for myself, I often laid in bed for extra hours, wondering *What's the use?* LinkedIn would still be on my computer whether I woke up at 4 a.m. or 9 a.m.—at least that is what I told myself.

Making up my routine was a bit of a shock to the system, albeit a subtle and quiet one. Note that I did not start out by mapping out my entire day. I did it gradually. And informally. But the more I did it, the more things I wanted to put into my day. I found myself not having enough hours to do the things I wanted to do. For the first time in months, I felt energized and even happy. Only a few weeks before, I languished in bed each morning, dreading having to leave it. Now I found myself excited to wake up each morning to greet the day. I became motivated and, above all, hopeful for the future.

I strongly recommend you set own structure as early in your unemployment period as possible. It will go a long way to fill the void left by the lack of long workdays, give you a sense of purpose, help you home in on your calling, and it could help you to heal.

## Strategies and Ideas for Routines

### Mindfulness

I used the word "mindfulness" in this chapter title for a reason. I told you that I had filled my days rather well. What I lacked were a focus and strategy. Those missing elements allowed me to easily ignore my routine. Having a goal will keep you focused. I set very small but very achievable goals early on in my routines. I had shelves of unread books, so I went through and picked a few that I wanted to read and set a goal of completing one a week. Some were about my profession. Some were classics, and some were pure unadulterated trash; I loved them all. Completing each one gave me a sense of accomplishment and completion I missed. The feeling of accomplishment made me feel good about myself and energized me to want to take on more projects to complete.

As I developed a strategy for my reading, I did so for my general routine as well. I actively sat down to write out what I wanted to come from my efforts. How did I want to develop and grow personally and professionally? This mindfulness made me focus on addressing the depression and anxiety that had been my loud and obtrusive roommates for the past six months. I looked for ways to calm them and incorporated those ways into my routine. I also looked around at where I wanted to be professionally and which professional accomplishments I had always wanted to achieve. Once I determined a few professional goals, such as obtaining my SPHR certification and learning more about Emotional Intelligence, I set about looking for free courses through the e-learning sites such as Coursera and the unemployment office. I also looked within my network to find people who could help and support me as I learned and developed.

As time went on and as I knocked down goals—and I cannot begin to tell you the rush I felt with each accomplishment—I added to my routine, one item at a time. Within a month, I had a very tight schedule of my daily tasks, which I did every day, even weekends. I scheduled in personal time. I scheduled time with friends. I scheduled time to do nothing. The difference was that I now had a reason to get up in the morning, and I found myself eager to go to bed each night, no longer as a means to escape reality but as a means to get rest to meet the upcoming day. I started to feel valuable and happy. Things I had not felt in a very long time.

## Your Resources and Environment

As you start to build your routine, be sure you are set up for success. If you choose to make running a start of your daily routine, make sure you have all the proper equipment first. If you choose to make reading every day a part of your routine, make sure you have a comfy and quiet place to read. If writing is your thing, do you have a laptop? Pen? Paper? If your environment and the needs of your routine are not in place, you risk failure. This is one of the reasons I suggest you add one item at a time. Once you have established a success and transition that goal to BAU, you can turn your attention to adding another item.

I do not have a dedicated office space in my home, but most of the goals I had set for myself involved writing, often on the computer. Luckily, I had a working laptop and was able to afford internet service. Also, as luck would have it, I had tons of blank journals, being a huge collector of them over the years, which served me well as I wrote. Before you choose a goal or set out to incorporate one into your routine, make sure your environment is conducive to your success.

## Family

In this chapter, I stress that you focus on yourself and practice extreme self-care, but by no means do I want you to exclude your family. Although I am single with no children, I understand that it is hard, if not impossible, to focus on yourself over your family. Your instinct will be to shower your family with time and attention since there will undoubtedly be a change in income and lifestyle. Try to view it this way: You are no good to anyone else unless you are at your best. Taking care of yourself right now does not mean you exclude your family entirely. It means you take care of yourself so you can take care of them.

Have an honest talk with your family/partner. Remember how I asked you to think of yourself as an entity and that you were really You, Inc.? Think of your family/partner as fellow employees or think of your family as Family, Inc., a partner organization of You, Inc.

Asking loved ones to support you in establishing a routine and in caring for yourself makes them active participants and will help people not to feel isolated from you. They'll be involved in your success. You will need their support, and they will need to feel as if they are supporting you. I have a client who is a single parent. Her children felt at loose ends and demanded her attention when she set time aside to reflect and work on her routine strategy. After we consulted, I suggested she ask her children to help her decide how to fill her time and come up with ideas not only for her but also for themselves. Her children fought for her attention because they felt left out. She had gone from hours of playing with them each day to trying to be alone in her bedroom to plan. This change in their routine left her children feeling unwanted and probably a little afraid, even though what she was doing was for the good of her family. By sitting down and having a talk with her children and asking for their help, she made them feel they were a part of the process. Now instead of hours of playtime, the children feel helpful and active participants in Mommy's success. They began to work together by taking walks together. This got everyone out of the house and active. She incorporated menu planning so that when they went grocery shopping, the children made a game of finding the right ingredients for a recipe and were more than happy to help cook. She even initiated a daily guided meditation that the children followed. She swears it had an extraordinarily calming effect on everyone. Her routines gave her structure, and more than anything else, they allowed her to focus on her needs without alienating her children.

Instead of walking on eggshells around her, the children understood that all of this was to help her be happier and focus on finding work. Instead of her unemployment being a silent issue, it became something she and her children felt comfortable discussing and proactive in facing.

Self-care, although it means focusing on yourself, does not mean isolating others in the process. If done correctly, it can become a unifying process for your family and an empowering and enlightening process for you.

## Money

When I talk to people about implementing extreme self-care, their first thought is often, *What will this cost me?* When you are out of work, and definitely have been out of work for a long time, money is a huge issue. Sometimes it feels as if it is your only issue. As you structure your mindful extreme self-care, look for things to do that do not cost money or that cost very little money. Do you have books you haven't read? Add reading to your routine. Donate your books to a charity when you are done, or clear a shelf or table for the ones you have read so you can revel in your accomplishment. Maybe you can't afford to join a gym, but is there a nice park or neighborhood where you can walk? What about home projects? Does your closet need cleaning? Do you have stacks of papers to sort through? All of these can be added to your routine and don't cost a thing.

## Apps

What did we do before phone apps became available to serve our every whim? Apps now schedule us, entertain us, and do things for us we never realized we needed. Look at your phone or one of the app stores to find ways to help your routine. Part of the beauty of apps is that so many of them are free if you don't mind sorting and sifting through some ads. Do you want to start a daily meditation? There are hundreds of apps for that. Want to read but have no books? Kindle or Nook are right there for you, and Kindle has thousands of free titles. As much as I love to hold a book in my hands, the siren song of free books on Kindle was more than I could handle. Some apps will provide walking paths and trails in your area. Apps for free podcasts. The list is limited to your imagination and search abilities. If you are stuck, Google "best free apps" for ideas, or better yet, ask your kids for help. You will be amazed at the world that opens up for you.

## YouTube

What if you can't get to the gym or afford one, or what if you have some home projects but need help? YouTube is free, again if you are willing to look at some ads. I could never motivate myself to go to the gym, a huge regret and mistake I made during my unemployment. I was able to find things such as yoga, guided meditations, and free professional development on YouTube. As a visual learner (I learn by watching, not by reading), this was ideal for me. Where it was most handy was in shoring up my computer skills, something I knew would be essential in reentering the job market. This came in especially handy as I applied to jobs that wanted candidates to have familiarity with certain software systems. I spent hours watching YouTube videos so that I could have informed discussions with hiring managers. More than once in the interview process, I was told my systems knowledge had propelled me to the next round of interviews.

## Rituals

The idea of adding a ritual to your routine may sound off-putting to some, and to others, it may be what you need to slip comfortably and mindfully into a routine. And that is the purpose of a ritual—to make the ordinary important and special. If using the term ritual bothers you, think of it as a kickoff or tradition. As you establish it, your routine will become a type of ritual you use to improve yourself and keep you on course. Rituals do not have to be long and drawn out. Plainly put, rituals are a set of actions or behaviors that we do before, during, and after events where we want the desired outcome.

The key to a successful ritual is that it is important to the person conducting it. You probably have a plethora of rituals that you already perform. Some people do not feel that their day is started without that first cup of coffee, enjoyed in a special chair in complete silence. Some end their day with a relaxing glass of wine. Sports fanatics live by ritual, practicing the same habits each game day that they did the day their team won the big game to help them win yet again.

There is now increasing scientific evidence that rituals go well beyond their surface appeal to help us improve performance. This does not mean that not washing your favorite sports jersey will help your team win the next game. However, performing a ritual before diving into your daily routine or before each day of work has been proven to jump-start your brain and positively influence performance. Here's an astounding fact—it doesn't even have to be a ritual of your choosing. In 2018 a study at the University of Toronto instructed participants to perform a set ritual before completing a task. Even though the ritual was assigned to the participants, they reported feeling less anxiety while completing the task. They had less feelings of failure when they didn't complete their tasks properly than their colleagues who were given no ritual and were asked to merely complete the same task. Rituals reduced their feelings of personal failure, thus improving or not detracting from their performance at a given task. Participants who chose their own ritual experienced an even greater loss of anxiety than their fellow participants assigned a ritual. In the sports world, it's called "choking" when athletes are so affected by an error that they cannot get past it. Rituals can help calm the brain under stress, increase confidence, and reduce the opportunity for error to negatively impact activity.

To increase your success with a ritual, it should be your own—a task or behavior that you believe in and that is simple and easy for you to repeat. It should have meaning for you. One of the easy things I have suggested to you is viewing your mission and vision statements each day as a reminder of what you are working towards. For my ritual, I began each day by meditating and envisioning myself back to work. Eventually, my entire routine became my daily ritual. Make your ritual your own, and you will be shocked at how it brings meaning to your life.

## Write Out Your Best Possible Life

A suggestion from the book *Creating Your Best Life* recalls a study where participants were asked to spend twenty minutes writing about their best possible life. They were encouraged to use positive words such as *happy, good, healthy*, etc. Participants in the study who wrote about their best possible life reported increased and higher levels of life satisfaction than the participants who did not do the writing exercise. The writing exercise can help you increase happiness factors, and also help you determine what makes you happy. Study participants reported that they began to see patterns and notice achievable goals in their writings over time that helped them determine what they truly wanted. Maybe you will write about spending more time with your family. Or maybe you will write about starting a new hobby or your own business. I suggest doing this on a daily basis. Initially, you might feel very self-conscious and fake doing the exercise. I encourage you to be as fanciful as you like. Eventually, your true self will come out. You may even find it hard to stop after twenty minutes. Keep going. Some of my writing from that exercise has become the basis for the business I am currently building.

## Vision Board and Primes

Vision boards are not for everyone, but many people find them to be a way to help them determine what they want in life. There is no right or wrong with vision boards except to make sure you put things you really like and want on it. Let the practical side of you think of this as a way to get rid of all of those old magazines and catalogs. This is also a fantastic activity to do with your kids/spouse/partner. A friend of mine now does this annually with her children and keeps their boards in their rooms. Once a month, the family looks at their boards to determine how close everyone is to the things they want. You can focus the board on getting a job, a family trip, or a new career path. There is no limit. Eventually, you might see patterns coming out about the type of work you are looking for.

There is actual science behind the idea of a vision board. All those signs with a picture of a stick figure throwing something in a trash can and those slides before a movie showing a finger pressed to the lips reminding us not to talk during the feature presentation have a name. They are called "primes." Primes are cues that trigger our brain and our body to do goal-oriented behaviors. The movie slide and litter sign are all there to trigger the appropriate behaviors. Vision boards can act the same way. If you have a picture of someone working out on your board, this is a cue for you to take on healthier behaviors. It is not a guarantee of things happening; however, it can help flip the switch to more productive action. Remember what your parents did with your artwork and report cards? Remember how good you felt whenever you had breakfast and saw a school test proudly displayed on the fridge with the Disney World magnet right as you were leaving for school each day. Guess what? Your parents were (probably) unknowingly setting you up with primes. Our parents are so much smarter than we give them credit for being.

## Bullet Journaling

I am trying to master the art of bullet journal, but the number one benefit for me was a sense of accomplishment. Bullet Journaling differs from traditional journaling. Traditional journaling tracks your emotions, hopes, dreams, feelings and is usually written in prose. Bullet journaling tracks accomplishments. *The Bullet Journal Method* describes a mindfulness/productivity system created by Ryder Carroll, a designer based in New York. In his words, the Bullet Journal is meant "to help you track the past, organize the present, and plan for the future." I kept my Bullet Journal list on my refrigerator so I could see the completed list.

I also strove to add a good behavior to the list every day to reinforce the habits such as "drinking 48 ounces of water a day," "one hour of reading," "taking vitamins." The act of checking things off on the Bullet Journal gave me a sense of accomplishment and served as a primer for me to continue good behaviors. Once, I took it down when friends stayed for the weekend and I slacked on behavior until I put it back on the fridge. There are special journals made for Bullet Journaling, but you can use regular grid paper as well. I used plain college rule paper and drew my own slightly misaligned grids and columns. Bullet Journals are often thought to be a series of lists, but nothing could be further from the truth. Knowing that pictures and creativity engages people, Bullet Journaling encourages users to follow their creative muses. Some of the journal examples I have seen are works of art. Users draw pictures to match what they are tracking. For example, if you wanted to count down the days to Christmas, you could draw a tree with each ornament standing for a day until the holiday. You could color in an ornament each day until the holiday. You could take the journaling/tracking to another level by drawing pictures of the gifts you want to give under the tree and coloring them in or drawing a box around each gift once you purchase it. There are no limits here. Bullet Journaling is effective because it forces users to be strategic, and to revisit what they have drawn regularly and take account of what they have accomplished and what they have yet to do. Where it succeeds is that users tailor it to their tastes and creativity, giving it a special meaning. At best, it is a fun and creative way of reaching goals. At worst (which isn't too shabby), it helps users determine and learn from their primes.

## Meditation

I struggled with this one. I have spent most of my life laughing at the practice of saying *Ommmmm* to achieve inner peace. I humbly admit I was wrong. This is one of the few practices that I did continue after I got a job, and it has never failed to center me. I now even refer to my guest bedroom as the Meditation Room because that was where I chose to meditate. On the days I was unable to do this, I felt anxious and restless. I was also astounded by the short amount of time needed each day to achieve calm. I cannot still my mind or body for long. My maximum meditation time is still twenty minutes. Usually, it is ten. I cannot overemphasize the positive impact that a ten-minute investment has on my well-being.

It may surprise you that meditation is rooted in science. The U.S. Army Research Laboratory ran a year-long study to determine the impact of mediation on the human body. The experiment focused on the impact mediation had on body stress. Stress has a severely negative effect on the body, particularly the heart. If a body is placed under constant long-term stress, the result can be irreparable damage to the heart leading to heart disease and high blood pressure. Although we cannot always change the stress we have, meditation can help us control its impact on our body by disrupting its negative effects on the human heart.

The Army Research study successfully tested a model for moderating the impact of stress on the heart and brain by measuring the impact brain activity had upon the functioning of the heart. The research team compared two schools of meditation and determined that yoga was effective in reducing stress. They also found that the long-term practice of meditation makes the positive physical changes of reduces stress permanently on the heart *if* meditation is used as a regular practice. The study also determined that people who regularly meditated showed a stronger ability to keep emotions in check. A further benefit of meditation was that participants in the study showed the ability to carry out goal-oriented behavior using complex mental processes and cognitive skills.

Although historically mediation has been used to alleviate stress, the Army Research Laboratory has also begun to investigate the impact mediation can have upon Post Traumatic Stress Disorder (PTSD), with promising results. Given that more often than not, when we lose a job, it is after a prolonged time of stress on the job, because of long hours, the signs of potential layoffs, or even unhappiness, someone having lost work is no doubt already suffering from a type of PTSD. Keep in mind that you have been dealing with being out of work and worrying about bills, family, and the anxiety, rejection, and the stress that come hand in hand with looking for work. That is a lot to take on. People returning to work often have PTSD. The practice of continued meditation after returning to work can help to assuage the symptoms of PTSD.

## Meet with Kindred Spirits

This act alone kept me sane. Surround yourself with people who make you feel good and who make you "up" your game. Try to find people who are in your situation. Start a Facebook group or check out your LinkedIn network. This will serve to get you out of the house. And might even help you find leads. A very dear friend of mine and a former coworker lost her job shortly after I lost mine. We made it a point to meet each other regularly to keep our spirits up and sound out job opportunities. Her work had given her a resource for finding new work—how to beef up your LinkedIn page, write your resume, etc. She gladly shared her resources with me, and I gladly gave her the name of the resume writing company I was using. We lifted each other up when we were down, and we celebrated for each other as we both finally regained employment.

One of my favorite movies is the 1997 British comedy, *The Full Monty.* In the film, a recession has hit a small town in England and put most of its men out of work. One loveable opportunist notices that townswomen scrape together enough money to see a Chippendales-style revue, even though money is tight. He looks around at his mates and decides to put together his own, albeit less sexy, revue to make the money he needs to keep seeing his son. One aspect of the film that is almost hidden is that the town has set up a club/gathering place where all unemployed people can gather. This is not an actual place for them to network but rather a place of camaraderie. It gets them out of the house. Together they play games and play cards, and eventually, they share their deepest fears as they bond. The hidden message in the film is that unemployment is an equalizer and that we as people need to interact with each other. A bunch of unlikely co-conspirators becomes friends and confidants. They learn from each other and depend upon each other. The revue happens to hilarious and financially beneficial results, but above all, these men bond. The friendships might not endure, but they have more than benefited each man as he finds the support he needs to get through one of the most challenging times in his life.

One of my saving graces was my friend Gigi. We looked for work together and helped keep each other sane. The key was that we were productive together even when we were apart. I lived in Annapolis, and she lived in D.C. One of my favorite things we did that got each other moving was what we affectionately called our Marie Kondo Contests. We each picked a room or project in our homes and set some boundaries. We took pictures of our before, during and after, and texted them to each other as proof. We cheered each other on and even brought out the occasional good-natured trash talk. Gigi is a dynamo, and she spurred me on. Often you are told to build your network with people who make you work harder, and Gigi definitely fits that bill in multiple categories. Everyone should have a Gigi.

## Gratitude

People from Oprah Winfrey to Justin Bieber have spoken about how a practice of gratitude has helped them get through dark times and made them grateful for the things they have. I incorporated this as a daily practice and made this one of the last things I did each night before bed. I found a special container, a crystal jar that I had given my mother when I was a child. I was touched that she kept it all those years, and I still treasure it. I found among my stored office supplies a pretty package of Post-it notes and a shiny gold Sharpie. I placed the jar in a special corner of my home, and each night before I went to bed, I write down the date and three things for which I was grateful. Sometimes, the list was not terribly profound. Other times, I wrote down the name of dear friends, and sometimes—often—I repeated things. The ritual made me realize that even though things were bleak, I still had so much going for me. I needed the reminder. On New Year's Eve, a few months after I had returned to work, I received results from a routine surgery. I had pre-cancerous cell growth in my uterus. I could not believe I had come through the prior year just for this to happen. That night I went through all the things that I wrote down that I was grateful for during the hard times. With great awe, I read on those notes the path of getting the call for a phone screen for my current job, getting the interview, getting the second interview, and then getting the offer. It was a reminder that good times and good news does happen. I realized if I got through the year of unemployment, I could get through my diagnosis. Sure enough, thanks to a great team of doctors and the proper treatment, I recently received a clean bill of health -- one more thing for me to be grateful for. I still keep this practice to this day.

What follows are a few items I felt would be essential for a routine. However, following these actions will go a long way to keeping you healthy and help you maintain a positive outlook.

## Tips to Keep Going

Being unemployed was one of the worst experiences of my life. It is sad and lonely and crushing to the human spirit. There are tiny little habits and tasks you can perform that will have an enormous impact on you.

**Sleep.** Get proper sleep. All too often, sleep can be a distraction and a refuge. Keeping a good sleep routine— at least eight hours and not more than ten—will keep you rested and on schedule. Do not try to alter your sleep schedule too much, and if at all possible, keep going to bed and waking up at the same time you always did. Try not to fall asleep in front of the TV, and do sleep in your bed. Body aches from the couch and a disturbed sleep pattern caused by television noise will not make you feel better.

**Diet.** When unemployed and without the discipline of a routine, it is easy to fall into bad eating habits, especially if you live alone. I ate most of my meals out of a box and over the sink. You must maintain a healthy diet—low on sugar and processed foods. Fast food is a particularly enticing trap because it is convenient, cheap, and comforting. A proper diet can be a challenge as you will be on a budget, and fresh foods cost more. We tend to seek comfort through food. Think more treat than indulgence. Reward yourself with a favorite food after completing a walk or successfully following your daily routine, rather than turning to food to feel better. Try your best, and at the very least, go easy on junk food and snacks. Having a balanced diet will help stave off feelings of depression. Consider an app such as *My Fitness Pal* to help you track your daily food. It will serve as a good and beneficial distraction during your day.

**Shower and Get Dressed.** If when you were working, you had the privilege of working from home, it was probably tempting to dress from the waist up. Most of my coworkers have taken casual to a new extreme during the COVID pandemic, and things such as makeup, shaving, and jewelry have gone the wayside. When I was out of work, I often spent days in the same pajamas or yoga pants. I committed to making sure I showered and got dressed every day. I am not suggesting you put on a suit each day, but even the effort of wearing your jeans will make you feel better. The longer you are unemployed, the easier it is all too easy to slack off in this department. Making this kind of effort will get you moving, which will only help you to feel better. Besides, if you get a last-minute call for an interview, at the very least, you want to be showered and ready to go with short notice. Otherwise, you risk missing out on The One.

**Get Out of the House.** I thought my friends were alarmist about me until one of them pointed out that I hadn't been out of the house in weeks. Changing your environment often can stave off feelings of loneliness and depression. As we move our bodies, we generate endorphins, the feel-good hormones.

## Sample Routine

My routine seldom stayed constant. It changed as I got job interviews and as I was able to get out more and more. The one thing that remained the same for several months was that I always had a plan for the day. Yours will vary, and it should reflect you and your needs and domestic situation.

Here is a sample of an average day for me. Yes, I do get up at 4 a.m., every day. I have no idea why, but I do. No, you do not have to do that. You do you.

| | |
|---|---|
| •4 a.m. | Wake Up |
| •4:15-4:35 a.m. | Writing Exercise: Your Best Possible Life (I did this virtually every day of that period). |
| •4:40-4:55 a.m. | Meditate. I used the app Calm until the free trial ran out and then switched to Deep Meditate, as it was free. |
| •5-6 a.m. | Read a book for self-development. They changed as time went on and as I completed each book. |
| •6:-7 a.m. | Send out resumes, mindfully |
| •7-8 a.m. | Read for pleasure, from an actual book |
| •8-9 a.m. | Read *The Artist's Way*, a self-development book I had been trying to get through for years. |
| •9-11 a.m. | Breakfast, housework, home projects |
| •11 a.m.-1 p.m. | Free time |
| •1-1:30 p.m. | Lunch |
| •2-3 p.m. | Send out resumes, network, etc. |
| •3-5 p.m. | Walking/yoga/gym (This was non-peak time at my gym.) |
| •5-6 p.m. | Free time |
| •6-6:30 p.m. | Dinner |
| •7-7:30 p.m. | Prep for the upcoming day |
| •8-9 p.m. | Journaling/writing |
| •9:30-10 p.m. | Bedtime prep |
| •10 p.m. | Bed |

## Tips for Developing a Successful Routine

Be mindful and strategic as you think out the items you want to put on your schedule.

- Choose a mixture. I structured my list to include mind, body, and soul and the essential life items, such as paying bills and of course, looking for work.
- Balance what you have to do and what you want to do.
- Include others such as family and friends. Let them know what you are doing, invite them to participate, and ask for support, suggestions, and help.
- Don't do everything at once. I added to my list, one item at a time.
- Make checklists, whether they are Bullet Journaling or a to-do list. Few things surpass the feeling of accomplishment than crossing something off as done.
- Prep your resources and your environment every day. Make sure you are set up for success.
- If you miss an item, do not beat yourself up. Try it again the next day. If you still have trouble getting your list complete, see what needs to be modified.

And finally…

### Proper Preparation

Journaling first thing in the morning became essential to my routine. Each night before I went to bed, I set myself up for success for the next day. I had cleared my dining room table, which, until I lost my job, had been the resting place for mail, magazines, and a virtual eyesore for months. Now it was a beautiful, clean workspace. I chose the dining room table because it was my favorite piece of furniture. I was saddened that I had so mistreated it. Now it would be the area for my success. Each night I lovingly placed my journals and laptop on the table, alongside pens I had found stored in a box.

I added to the table the current self-help book I was working on. I then went to the living room and made sure my reading area was adequately set up, with my book placed on the table next to my favorite chair. I made sure that for every item on my routine, I was set up and ready to complete it the next day. I removed the excuse of looking for a blanket to wrap around me on a cold day—it was already there in the comfy chair. I thought through the morning's need for fresh coffee by setting up the coffee maker. If I were walking that day, I made sure all my gear was clean and ready to go before bed. In other words, I made sure I had nothing to deter me from following my activities. I want you to do the same. As I walked through my house setting up my activities for the next day, I felt accomplished and empowered, knowing I had completed the day's tasks and was set up to do the same tomorrow. This made me feel happy, which calmed anxiety and removed depression. It changed my entire outlook on my unemployment. I began to look at this time as a gift to work on myself—just as I want you to do. Remember when I asked you to set aside your interview clothes and to look at them every week? I was helping you set up a prime. Do this for yourself to accomplish your daily goals.

You do not have to plan every second—that was a personal choice for me. You should also make sure that you weave in some flexibility for unexpected events and those all-important interviews. But you should also tenaciously guard your routine because your health and peace of mind might depend upon it.

## Celebrate your accomplishments!

You may not feel that you have anything to celebrate, but I encourage—no, insist—that you take the time to celebrate your daily accomplishments. Think of it as tiny dry runs for when you celebrate returning to work. I celebrated my days in numerous ways. Sometimes I indulged in a movie. Other times, I opened a nice bottle of wine I had been saving. As money became tighter, more often than not, the celebration was a nice long hot bath before bed. Toward the end, I got quite pruney. Your celebration does not have to be elaborate, and it does not have to cost you money. I have a client who celebrates each daily to-do list by placing it in his shredder. I hope he plans to use the result as confetti when he returns to work!

It is important to celebrate your wins because celebrations serve as a reminder that you have accomplished something. Celebrating gets your adrenaline running, which makes you feel better. You get into the habit of recognizing your accomplishment. Better, if you have loved ones living with you (or not), bring them into the celebration so they can see the progress of You, Inc.

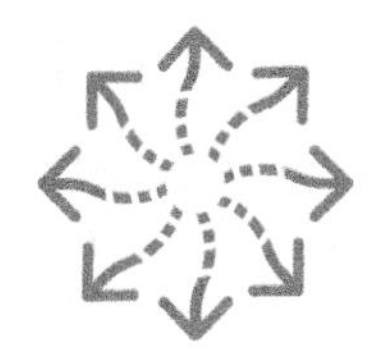

# 7
# HELPING OTHERS

This is a topic that came up as one of my friends was proofing this book for me. This person had been an amazing friend who gave me a shoulder to cry on and kept my spirits up. I was shocked when they said that the whole year I was unemployed, they had no idea what to do for me or how to treat me. I appreciated their honesty and wished they had said something earlier. When a friend loses a job or goes through any loss or difficulty, people know how to initially react—usually with great empathy. However, as time goes on, people no longer know how to behave. They go through myriad emotions. You almost feel helpless as you watch a friend suffer. And if you are that friend who is suffering, like I was, you feel everything from abandonment to anger at those around you. This is not only because of what you are going through but also because of how you are being treated.

How other people treat you is a reflection of them and what they are going through, not a reflection of you. If you are feeling distanced from friends through this period, understand that it reflects them and the things they might be feeling or handling during this time. Because the purpose of this book is to help you through your period of unemployment, I thought it important to take some time to discuss the reactions of your friends and colleagues toward you during this time.

Why do we hesitate or refuse to help others when it is entirely within our power to do so? If I could answer this, I would hold one of the keys to the universe, but I think it boils down to how we handle our fears. There is so much that goes into why we fear. Fear is a primal emotion, a survival instinct with physical and psychological dimensions. Fear is meant to protect us from others and ourselves. Fear can be our gatekeeper and babysitter, our protector, and our guide. It can also be a symptom of other things, such as our anxiety and stress. Fear can be partly animal instinct and partly taught lessons. We all experience it in different ways and react to it in different ways. Our hearts race, our emotions shut down, we avoid, we attack.

Fear is not a bad thing. Fear has a co-conspirator, resistance. Resistance is not as great as fear. It is defined as an action that results in us withstanding or defying or opposing someone. Often the two are confused. Fear is the instinct or feeling, and resistance is that action resulting from fear. When we fear something, we tend to resist it. You can overcome both, but you have to reflect and discover their root cause.

I know from first-hand experience how difficult it is to deal with unemployment, especially if you are without family or a partner. If you are without a close family or a significant other, your friends, in essence, become your surrogate family. Given the strong need for support while out of work, distance from friends can feel like being abandoned by family. A few friends gave me feedback that they were afraid they would not have the bandwidth to support my needs. Later what many admitted was that they anticipated an event that had not happened.

This often occurs with fear: Our instincts and reflexes kick in, and we protect ourselves and our own, even when there is no track record to justify our expectations. It happens for a host of reasons. My advice to your friends and even family is taking care of your oxygen mask, but also make sure that you look to help others once you have done so. It is up to each person to communicate and be honest about what they can and cannot do.

As the person who was out of work, all I can tell you is not to take it personally if you lose some friends along the way. I know how hard this is. You will be hurt at a time in your life when you cannot afford to be hurt, when every transgression and slight is magnified a million times over. You have lost part of your identity in losing your job, and you might lose another part of your identity defined by your friends and the company you keep.

The loss of even one friend feels as if someone in your life has died. Even now, I look back on the absence of a few friends from my life, and I mourn these friendships. There is still a wound, a hole that I am sure will never be filled. I had one dear friend I thought of as a sister -- a kindred spirit. We worked together and became close. Her family came to my home for Thanksgiving. I even stayed at her house and watched her children while she went on a business trip. I cared so much how this woman regarded me that I was ashamed to tell her I had lost my job. It was months before I could tell her. She completely cut me out of her life after that. The irony is that just as I was re-identifying myself, she lost her job. I did reach out. I received one or two texts, and that was all. Months later, a mutual friend reached out and said that my friend didn't return my calls because she felt so ashamed of how she treated me, and now karma was coming for her. This is a reflection of her.

An irony is that we as human beings need each other, but we rarely discuss what we want and need. I encourage anyone on either side of a job loss to communicate what you are thinking, feeling, and needing. Respect what the other is going through, own your thoughts and actions, and do not blame anyone else for them.

There are legitimate reasons that we act the way we do in these difficult situations. One of them is survivor guilt, a severe condition that happens when someone has escaped a catastrophe. They do not have to know those who suffered or died but just have gone through the same situation or a relatively similar one. People who survived the 2017 Las Vegas massacre at the Mandalay Bay Resort, the 9/11 attacks, war—any tragedy—have reported going through this. They wonder why they were spared when others were not. They often feel unworthy of having survived. People deal with this in different ways. But survivor guilt is not just felt by those who have experienced tragedy—there is a ripple effect among the law enforcement officials who aid in the disaster and the hospital workers who help those injured in the disaster. Even someone who just views the story on the news may have these feelings. How people deal with guilt is influenced by their psychological profile. Survivor guilt used to be its own psychological disorder but is now considered a symptom of Post-Traumatic Stress Disorder as a means of widening the scope of the condition and the range of symptoms.

The symptoms of survivor guilt come in a vast range and intensity. They can include nightmares, depression, irritability, avoidance. They can also directly result in a survivor being afraid that if their friend has gone through a tragedy, then they too will experience the same tragedy. Those on the edge of survivor guilt go through their own evaluation of their life—questioning the choices they have made and even pivoting their paths and futures.

This is one of the reasons we often end up losing friends, or our friends create a distance between us after we go through a tragedy. Often, they are caught in their guilt or fear of being struck by our tragedy, such as being unemployed, or they already have their anxiety around their jobs and being near someone who has lost a job is a trigger for that anxiety, regardless of whether or not that anxiety is real or perceived. A large part of the problem is that the person experiencing the guilt doesn't understand what is happening—their human instinct of self-protection kicks in and they naturally defend themselves.

I found that after I lost my job, the friends who continued to stay with me were the ones who had already gone through their rite of passage of having lost and then regained employment. For the most part, these were individuals who had a happy and healthy home life with a huge support system. Most were financially secure. I had one friend, Alicia, whom I had considered a close friend. We shared similar backgrounds and had gone through similar experiences at the same company. Initially, Alicia was a rock after I lost my job, inviting me to dinners for which she picked up the check and even inviting me to her family's Thanksgiving dinner that year. We had planned to attend a conference together that January, and I was on the fence about attending. Another friend had used her airline miles to pay for my flight, but I was not comfortable spending the money on my hotel room. For Christmas, Alicia gave me a tiny little gift and a lot of cash, saying that she wanted to attend the conference with me. Alicia had just received a well-earned promotion.

Shortly after the conference, Alicia began to tell me that the promotion was not all it could and should have been. From what little detail she was telling me, it was eerie how much it reflected the things I had experienced right before I left my job. My heart bled for Alicia, but I also noticed her calls, emails, and texts became fewer. At first, I attributed it to the responsibilities of the new job. Eventually, they dwindled almost to radio silence. This happened around the same time a bunch of other friends also distanced themselves from me. Upset, I started to chalk it up to my having that disease of no one wanting to be around an unemployed loser.

I was pleasantly surprised when Alicia reached out to me in the summer. We met for a very cautious brunch where she admitted that she had placed the distance between us. I had no idea her role in the company was so hard. She was working around the clock, running just to stand still. What had been a game-changer in her life was that she had a new relationship, something positive that made her realize what was important to her. I told her I was hurt, but I also understood. We both made more of an effort not to have more frequent conversations but more meaningful ones. She ended up leaving her job. I find that I have more bandwidth to give her, having weathered the storm. This raises an important question. Why should I help someone if it might be detrimental to me? Again, the oxygen mask. I am not suggesting that you do anything at your peril. But I am asking you to consider it. It is often by helping others that we get past our own pain and issues.

In his book *Start with Why,* Simon Sinek mentions the impact of oxytocin. It is a hormone that creates intimacy and trust, the feeling that someone will protect you. Moms, babies, lovers feel this when they are protected and loved. Its secretion brings about a sense of safety. Oxytocin is powerful stuff. It is a very interesting chemical and has just as much influence on the giver as it does on the receiver. It also has an impact on the observer. This creates trust and safety for everyone. Just the simple act of doing a good deed increases the flow of oxytocin in your brain, creating a feeling, in layman's terms, of feeling good about yourself. It also prompts oxytocin to flow in the receiver's brain. What I find the most interesting is that if someone observes this act, the flow of oxytocin in *their* body increases, even if they do not know the giver and receiver of the good deed. Pretty powerful stuff, and yes, this can be one of the things that dig us out of the trenches of our survivor's guilt and depression. What are the little things that you can do for someone to begin that oxytocin reaction?

The first step, of course, is to do what you feel comfortable with. If you have guilt or have other things you need to focus on, I will say honesty will be one of the best things you can do for that friend. If you really are going through things and don't have the bandwidth to have conversations into the wee hours of the morning, then don't offer. Once Alicia had come clean with everything, I was able to reset my expectations of her. I now find myself in a reversal of fortunes. I had already told you of one friend who lost her job, and other friends have also lost their jobs since I resumed work. I now find myself in the position of paying it forward. And I, too, grapple with feelings of guilt that I have a job and with fear that the pandemic could cause me to lose it. I also am still suffering the effects of my year of unemployment, trying to recover on multiple fronts. I also know what it is like to be on the receiving end of being "cut out" from a friendship and hope never to make a friend replicate my own challenging experiences in being distanced. Here are some effective ways to help your friend who is out of work. They are simple actions capable of making a world of difference to them.

## Network

First and foremost, your friend needs a job. If your company is looking for a new manager of widgets and this is your friend's specialty, offer to talk with someone in HR to recommend them. If you are not comfortable with that, you shouldn't be friends with this person. Sorry, someone had to say it. If your friend contacts you and you are two degrees of separation from them and someone at ABC Corporation who happens to need a widget expert, offer to make an introduction.

Offer to read their resume and offer your professional opinion. One friend of mine sent out a blast email to all her HR contacts to see if they needed anyone in my line of work. No one had anything at my level, but I was able to expand my professional network by ten percent, resulting in a couple of leads.

## Get Them Out of the House

My friends were awesome about helping me do this. I was invited over for pizza nights, out for coffee, and asked to co-volunteer on projects. All of which allowed me to hang out with my friends and to keep busy.

## Little Things

Keep in mind that your friend is out of work, and so the little luxuries of your life are probably not a part of theirs. The little things you take for granted are probably things they have given up to save money. You would be shocked at the impact a tiny little gift has on a person's mental state. Out of the blue, someone I barely knew sent me a Starbucks gift card. His note said, *Sabina, I know you have a habit of being early for everything. Use this card to buy yourself a coffee as you wait for a job interview that will come soon.* First of all, I was touched by what he did. To this day, I have no idea how he knew I lost my job. We were not particularly close, although I would say we were cordial colleagues. I was touched that he recalled my slightly annoying habit of arriving early to meetings. Every time I used that card —and imagine my shock when I learned there was $50 on it—I thought of this coworker with gratitude. Oxytocin. I used the card to buy myself a coffee or water only before an interview and walked into each meeting energized by this person's belief in me. A coffee gift card has since become part of a care package I put together whenever I hear that a friend has lost their job.

## Gas Cards

This was a lifesaver my friend Mary gave to me just as I was starting my current role. She handed me a $50 gas card, saying she had it lying around the house. I know that is not true. But it was so sweet that she realized you have to have gas in your car to get to work and to get to interviews. I cannot overstate how much this meant to me, and it meant even more because she was out of work at the same time I was looking for a job. I knew she was going through her crisis of faith, yet she still took a moment and some of her limited funds to do something for me.

## Grocery and Food Cards

You have a lot of options in this realm, thanks to the internet. For over two months, anonymous bags of groceries showed up at my house, and as a result, my pantry was usually stocked full of things I would have never bought while out of work. It seemed like a tiny miracle. I got a small steak with all the fixings. I got a bag that contained coveted Manchego cheese and arborio rice just when I wanted to try my hand at making paella. I later learned that a friend of mine had been viewing my Pinterest page (I had lots of time to daydream) and had one of the grocery services deliver ingredients that mirrored my pins so I could treat myself and also experiment as a chef. Such a sweet and thoughtful thing to do.

## Other Gift Cards

Friends spoiled me with cards to the movies, cards for Visa, and a few local restaurants. Most of these cards came from people who did not reach out to me regularly. It took me a while to realize that this is how this contingent of my friends showed support because, for various reasons, they either didn't know what to say or could not spare the emotional bandwidth. Sometimes you have to realize that support is support. It may not be what you need, but you have to give the other person credit for their efforts.

## Beyond Money

Money is not the only way you can help a friend. Once I was able to start structuring my days, I made reading a huge part of things. My goddaughter is such a voracious reader that I often think words are really the only food she needs to survive. At Christmas, I suggested reading the classic *Rebecca* with her. I think she went along with it just to make me happy. After that, we began our little book group, and like most things on this list, it served to get me to interact with others. This, I am happy to say, is a practice that we have continued to this day.

## Exercise

Exercise is another area where I should have done better and where accountability and a friend can make all the difference. A dear friend constantly asked me to go on walks, and I am pretty sure I was quite snippy in my refusals. Be persistent. Ask your out-of-work friend to help you lose weight, make them feel obligated. Or offer to go to a local park and see where it goes from there. Don't force the issue, but who knows where it might lead for both of you?

## Change of Scenery

In April of 2019, my mentor finally put her foot down and said that I needed to come for a visit. She had been asking me to visit for months, and I kept putting it off. I live in Maryland, and she lives along the Gulf of Mexico. She had offered to fly me down to visit using her airline miles. Her thought was that I needed a warm climate to feel better, and she used the excuse of helping me recover from walking pneumonia as the impetus for the trip. Since I would stay in her home, there were few other expenses. I really couldn't say "no." She not only arranged for my ticket, but thanks to airline miles, she flew me first class. Besides giving me a safe place to stay, she used my visit to have a heart-to-heart with me about what I should do with my life. Let's call it what it was, an intervention of sorts. She has sometimes been more the driver for this book and other ventures that have come out of it than I was. She was right that a change of scenery did me good.

I realized we don't all have Fairy Godmothers like her (which is a crying shame), but most of us can offer a friend a safe change of venue to get them out of the house and give a break from their "normal." My visit served to break me from the spiral I had gone down and made me think about how to approach my job search differently, with productive and positive results. Sometimes we all need a little well-intended "kick."

Chapter 7

## Setting Expectations

There are dozens if not hundreds of ways to show support to your friend who is out of work. It does not have to be financial, nor should it be something that causes you stress and anxiety. The most important and significant thing you can do for a friend in this situation is to set a boundary with them. And this is a two-way street. You both have to have an important and crucial conversation about your wants and needs. And it will probably take multiple conversations and resetting boundaries. Letting someone know what you can and cannot do is as important as letting someone know what you need. Remember what Andy Storch advised us about it being OK for people to say "no." Hopefully, you will know which of your friends to turn to. But in the end, you both have to respect each other's needs. You and your relationship will be stronger for it. And don't forget to pay it forward when your fortunes reverse.

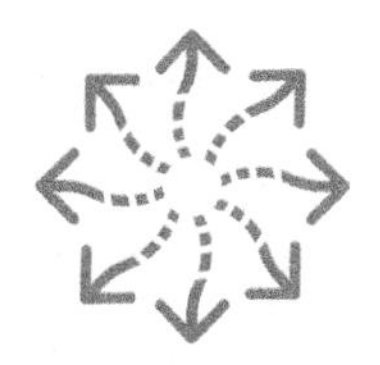

# 8
# INTERVIEWING

I debated about adding a section in this book about interviewing. Not because I didn't think the book needed or warranted it, but because there is so much out there already about the subject. I decided I would be remiss if I didn't include it. From start to finish, interviewing is by far the hardest part of the unemployment process. I would rather ask my friends for money or do without amenities such as hot water than have to be back on the interview carousel. Losing a job is hard enough, but putting yourself through the process, again and again, can be disheartening. It is, at times, overwhelming. It can be depressing, and it can erode already delicate self-esteem. Even the most confident of us waver a little at the thought of having to put ourselves out there. It is worse than going on a first date. There is pressure, judgment, excitement, and, more often than not, rejection. But worse than that is having to start the process all over again. I feel anxious just typing about interviewing.

The reality is that it is something we have to do, like it or not. My goal in this section is to get you through it as painlessly and as successfully as possible. Just as with everything else we have covered, I want you to rethink interviewing. I made it a point to go on every interview that was offered to me. Even if I knew the job was not going to be the right fit. At the very least, these interviews allowed me to network and continue to determine what I was looking for in a job and career. They helped me get over my anxiety about interviews. The less interested I was in a job, the less stress I felt interviewing for it. This let me build skills such as selling myself, responding to behavioral interview questions, and "closing the deal," an area where I felt my interview skills needed work. Interviewing got me out of the house. It also helped me learn what the job and salary expectations were for my field. And before you voice a concern about my wasting a company's time by interviewing for roles I didn't want, I will point out that one such interview led the recruiter and me to realize that although I was not a good fit for the job, they also had a need for a temporary learning consultant role—which I was given on the spot. Four months after another interview where I was unsure about the role, a company contacted me to offer me another job. I declined because I had already taken a full-time position. My point is that if a recruiter or a hiring manager sees something in you and calls you in for an interview, go! You never know what you will learn or what will come out of the interview.

## Some Pre-Interview Tips

### Be Polite

My biggest advice to you is to remain professional to anyone and everyone tied to the recruitment process. You just never know where anyone will end up or when you will reencounter them. How you carry yourself is a reflection of you, not the company where you are interviewing. You never know who is sharing your elevator, who is in the bathroom at the same time as you, or even who is in line behind you at the coffee place downstairs from your interview. I guarantee you that receptionists, office workers, and security all tell hiring managers if you are less than courteous with them. And it will count against you.

## Technology

Make sure your technology is ready. This means that you have a working cell phone, laptop, and Wi-Fi. You need to be available as soon as possible when a recruiter calls. Make sure that you have the equipment necessary to attend video meetings—and no, FaceTime is not acceptable. You need to be able to use platforms such as GoToMeeting, Zoom, Microsoft Teams, etc. And always, always test the links that recruiters send to you—well before your meetings start—to make sure their platform is compatible with your equipment.

## Look Professional

I was not kidding when I suggested setting aside your interview clothes almost immediately after losing a job. I have been in a situation where I was told that the hiring manager could see me that day, and I didn't have a thing to wear. I had to swing by Macy's and pray that I could find a reasonably priced interview suit that would fit appropriately, and that my credit card would not be rejected so I could wear it out of the store directly to an interview. Not exactly a confidence-builder. Also, today, there is an expectation that you will have to video interview for at least a portion of the process. Given that you are out of work, most organizations will expect you to do this almost immediately if key staff in the interview process are free. You need to be ready on their schedule, not yours. And don't for a second think you can get away with just wearing the mullet of interview outfits—business on the top and sweats on the bottom. I know of more than one candidate who was asked to stand for the camera. This was a test to see how seriously they took the interview. I hope we have evolved enough over the past couple of years that those sorts of tactics no longer occur, but don't take the chance. Besides, being fully dressed will give you a feeling of confidence that will come across favorably in an interview. I also know of a candidate who blithely went through an interview answering question after question only to be asked a final question: "By the way, we do require that our employees come to work fully dressed. Can we assume you will not be wearing pajama bottoms into the office?" Surprisingly, he did get the job. But let's not take any unnecessary chances. Always be ready.

## Act Professionally

We already prepared you for this with your Interview Kit. Make sure you dress professionally and that you act that way as well. Use proper names. Don't chew gum. Make sure your cell phone is off. Not on vibrate, but *off*. Say "please" and "thank you." Hold open doors for people. Make small talk but do not get too personal. This is work, after all. Be on time, but not too early. Above all, be patient.

## Additional Notes

Keep track of where you apply and who you spoke with, when, and where. The online application process makes it tempting to depend on the platform on which you apply for the job to be your database for following up. I would suggest not doing that. It is hard to keep track of multiple job search sites, and some of their tracking can be undependable. I recommend putting everything into a spreadsheet (such as Excel or Google Sheets) so that you can track all your steps, including when and where you apply and can add your notes. This will help with follow-up, and reviewing it will help you coach yourself in the interview process.

## The Process

In most cases, the interview process will follow a familiar pattern, but the steps vary depending upon the job level you applied for. The job level and salary (as well as the size of the company) will influence the length of time the interview process takes and the number of steps and people you will have to see. For the most part, however, the pattern will be:

- Apply for a job.
- Receive an email, text, or phone request for an initial phone screen, or sometimes for a video call.
- Undergo phone screen/video screen.
- Undergo in-person or video interviews with a hiring manager or sometimes, recruiter.
- Undergo a day of interviews with various stakeholders or a panel interview with stakeholders. Sometimes this step acts as a screening process, especially if the hiring manager is considered high up in the organization.
- Present to a panel if you will teach or present in the role you're applying for. Some companies ask for this step because it gives stakeholders who are making the hiring decisions the opportunity to see how you will "show" for the company. Sales positions often have this requirement.

Companies run their process differently, and there is no legal requirement for a process or the time it should take. I have been through all of the phases and will share some background tips on how to prepare for each phase. There is no set period in between any of these steps or for the whole process. You might have to keep in mind that many factors impact the interviewing timeline, such as holidays, conferences, and crucial times in the business. For example, if you were applying for a position at an accounting firm, it is unlikely staff would interview you in March or April because that is tax season. In the summer, people who are part of the interview process may be on vacation, which will impact the time the process takes. My experience has been that the process usually takes four to eight weeks from start to finish, depending on the number of steps. There is a call for organizations to do better at this, and I hope they hear it. I have seen an organization lose a top candidate because that person received another offer quicker. For those of us who are unemployed, every second count. Be patient and keep looking. Having more than one option will not only add to your confidence while interviewing, but will also give you practice and options. If an interview doesn't go your way, it is far less disappointing if you have a backup.

## Applying for the Job

Being unemployed is hard—one of the hardest things you will ever do. If you get to the end of your rope and your bank account, you will take anything that gives you an income and gives you value. But I caution you, please only apply for jobs for which you are truly qualified and willing to do long term. This is to save you heartache and to save the recruiter, who has one of the most challenging jobs in HR because they have to go through the bulk of the resumes they receive.

Also, do not apply to a job solely because you like the title. Companies like to put their own spin on things, and titles can get confusing in the global business environment. **Read the job description to make sure that this is something you genuinely want to do.** Make sure that you have the bare minimum requirements for a job or that you will have them shortly. For example, if you are finishing up your last semester of a bachelor's degree and the job requires you to have a diploma, apply, and quickly inform the recruiter that although you do not have the degree in hand, you will have it within a few months. This is to save face and heartache all around.

Often when you apply for a job, you will get a form letter thanking you for the resume. Do not reply to that letter. Your reply will go out into the ether or a spam folder. It is an automatic response letter generated by recruiting software. No one monitors that mailbox. It is a nice courtesy that lets you know that they received your resume. Nothing more.

## The First Connection

When an organization calls for a phone screen, they are checking for a few things. They want to be sure that you are you. Or rather, that you are the person from your resume. They may ask you some technical questions or try to get a feel for your job knowledge. This is to see if they want to invite you to continue in the hiring process. A recruiter's job is to find the best available candidates for a role. And that is what they are doing. When someone reaches out to you to set up a phone screen, there are a few rules. First, respond promptly. You are not dating the recruiter. There is no need to act coy. And I can guarantee that you are not the only person they have called. At this stage of the hiring process, recruiters will reach out to as many qualified candidates as possible so that they can screen from a large candidate pool. A savvy recruiter will speak with as many people as possible in this phase to be sure they are truly picking the best of the best to move forward in the process. Another rule is to be prepared. Sometimes a recruiter will call and want to speak at length right away. Other times, they are hoping to get your voicemail so they can leave a message about wanting to talk to you at length.

When you call back, know your availability, so you're ready if they want to set up a time to talk at length. Give at least two options for your availability but no more than three. Anything more than three or anything overly complicated will come off as disorganized and inefficient. If you leave a voicemail, be succinct and to the point. Leave the times when you are free to talk and thank them for reaching out to you. If you return an email, you have a little more freedom. When you respond, make sure that you are to the point and try to show that you know a little bit about the role and the company:

*Good afternoon (use their name as they signed their initial message to you—first name, last name, etc.),*

*Thank you for reaching out to me. I am extremely happy to be hearing back from Innovative IT as the Lead Code Writer position is just the type of job I am looking for. I am seeking a job that will allow me to use my prior experience as a consultant for an innovative international company that also has a desire to protect the environment.*

*I am free to discuss the role on the following days and times. Please let me know which works best for you:*

*Tuesday 9-12 EST*
*Wednesday 10-4 EST*
*Friday 11-3 EST*

*I look forward to hearing back from you and to discussing things further.*

*Sincerely,*
*Steven Bing*

Be patient. Recruiters have a ton of people to call, not only for the job you are applying but also for the other roles they are trying to fill. It may take a day or two for them to get back to you. Recruiters might not get back to you at all, especially if they have already found a number of qualified candidates. Do not take it personally. A lot of recruiters, particularly those who work at larger companies, are playing a numbers game. They are logging how many people they have reached out to, and they are going to move forward with only a certain number of qualified candidates who may fit the company culture for the next step. This is why it is essential to respond as soon as possible and with a flexible schedule. You will not look desperate. You will look efficient and interested.

Once you have a set time to speak with the recruiter, make sure you are organized. Have your resume handy, and if possible, have your LinkedIn page up. Recruiters worth their salt will have looked you up on LinkedIn, and no, you won't know it. They will probably have a membership option with LinkedIn so that their views are not visible to candidates—otherwise, they would be inundated with calls every time they looked at a profile. You will need all your information handy so that you can quickly refer to things and answer questions the recruiter asks you. When you speak with the recruiter, be sure that you are in a quiet place with good a cell phone or Wi-Fi reception so that you can both hear each other. Be ready a few minutes before the call. (I have had recruiters call early, and I have had recruiters call late.) And no, you cannot call them—they will contact you. Please do not ask otherwise. If you are meeting a recruiter on a conference line or a video call, be a minute or two early to make sure you can access the line or virtual meeting room.

Having a screening callback with a company means that you have met the minimum requirements of the role. This is good news because it means you have passed the first test. The initial screening is for the recruiter to get the feel of whether you really have the qualifications for the role and maybe see if you might be a personality match for the team, hiring manager, and the organization itself. A company would never hire an introverted salesperson, for instance. This screening is a test, albeit a very minor one. Chances are you are one of fewer than ten people they are considering, and they will probably narrow the field down to no more than five to come in for an interview. So far, so good. In the initial screening, be yourself. You want to be sure this role is a good fit for you, as well as you for it. Make sure you have one or two questions for the recruiter about the position and the company. (I am taking for granted that you have followed prior advice and applied only to jobs for which you are qualified and which you truly want. That means you have thoroughly researched the company before you apply for the job). Asking for a description of the working style of the hiring manager and the team is a good idea. Asking about the vision or mission of the company is also good.

It is always good to ask the recruiter questions as well. It shows you have researched the company and that you feel for how the role works within the organization's mission and vision. Some great and applicable follow-up questions include:

- What are the general responsibilities of the role?
- Can you tell me about the company's culture?
- What is the leadership style of the hiring manager?
- What is your favorite aspect of working here?

You don't need to ask a lot here—this is not the interview. You are trying to show that they should want you to come in for an interview. In these questions, you are showing curiosity about the role, company, and manager -- all good things.

Other questions to ask if you sense things are going well:

- What are the next steps in the process?
- Do you have a time estimate of when I will hear back from you?
- How quickly do you need to fill the position?

Remember: This is the initial call. If you are not moving forward as a candidate—if you hear back from them at all—it will probably be an email telling you that they have chosen to move forward with other candidates. Sometimes that is hard to hear. Look at it this way: You have gotten to practice on someone, and the role was probably not the right fit for you.

## The Next Round

Maybe you are one of the lucky ones, and you aced the phone interview and are going on to the next round. In today's world, this could be anything from another phone call with a hiring manager or senior recruiter to coming in for an in-person interview. My friend Tim referred to the entire interview process as if it were the television show *The Bachelor*. Moving forward after a phone screen was akin to "receiving the first rose." The next round of interviews was always referred to as the "group date." If you go to this phase, make sure you are adequately prepared. A recruiter will probably call you or email you, and this time they will give you a selection of days and times that work for the interviewer. I cannot emphasize how important it is that you respond as quickly as possible. You are not the only one they are contacting—this is, after all, the group date—and people are busy. I once missed out on a job I was qualified for because I was unavailable for the offered interview times. The one time on their calendar for which I was free got snapped up by another candidate before I could return their call. Just like that, I was left out of the process. It stung because I knew better than to wait to return a call from a recruiter. Return that phone call or email quickly. Claim your spot.

## Secondary Phone Call

Each company and organization runs its recruiting and interview cycles differently, so at this stage, there is no predictable workflow. A secondary phone call could be anything from a "look-see" from the hiring manager to determine if they want you to come in for a formal interview to a second vetting from someone in recruiting. It might even be a video call. Either way, look at it as a good thing that you have been asked to move on in the process, or as my friend, Tim, would say, the coveted one-on-one date.

The same rules as the initial phone call apply. You should respond as quickly as possible, and you need to be prepared. If you are speaking with a senior recruiter, look them up on LinkedIn. Have more detailed questions for them about the role and the organization. Unless you are seeking a position in HR and recruiting, you do not need to ask them about themselves. However, this would be a great time to ask what the hiring manager is looking for and any other questions you have about the process and the organization. Do your homework.

## In-Person Interview

You have aced all the screening interviews, and all those in recruiting feel comfortable forwarding you for an in-person interview. The objective in this phase is to sell yourself, convince the person(s) interviewing you that you are the right person for the job, and make sure that you believe this role and this organization is the right fit for you.

All companies handle their interview process differently. Sometimes it is an interview with the hiring manager, and that is all. Other times, there is an interview "layer" in between you and the hiring manager meant to do many things, such as filter candidates for a further round of interviews or make sure that the prospective candidate will be a good match for the entire team or a collaborating department. This can be true if you are interviewing at an organization that relies upon peer teams and collaboration. Organizations handle team interviews in many different ways. Sometimes it will be a case of the candidate meeting individually with team members. If the team has not been well prepared in the interview process the candidate, may feel as if they are consistently being asked the same questions repeatedly by different team members. Sometimes it is a panel interview where a team sits on one side of a table and you the other. It can sometimes feel like you are facing a firing squad or a tribunal. Regardless of the method, the team's job is to let a hiring manager know if they think you are qualified and see if they think they can work with you.

Keep several things in mind. If you weren't qualified, you wouldn't be there. On paper and through the phone screenings, it has been determined that you have passed muster. This group is really seeing whether you fit in with the team's culture and work practices. This is to benefit you as much as them. Do not think or feel that you need to prove to them that you are worthy. That thought could make you come across as needy or desperate. Everyone there knows you want or need a job, and they know that you are qualified, or else you would not have made it to the in-person interview stage. Be confident (and you should be, as you have made it through to the "hometown visit" of the process) and knowledgeable about the organization, and you are halfway there.

If they are doing things right, a panel will ask you the same series of questions they have asked every other candidate. This might come off as a little unengaged or bored, especially if you are the last interview of the day. (Always try to book for a morning appointment). Organizations should ask all candidates the same questions to bring a level of fairness to the process. If an organization has really thought about its recruiting process, most of the questions you will be asked will be behavioral-based; each question is crafted to find out how you behave under specific circumstances. Very well-crafted recruiting processes tie these questions into the organization's values or mission statement. They want to see the degree to which you fit into the company's culture. Any shrewd interviewer will be able to pick up on your responses and interpret them and will have some follow-up questions ready. It is best to answer questions using a balanced statement stating the cause and the effect. Let the interviewer know what you did and the impact of your actions. If you need clarification, ask for it. An interviewer will take it as a positive sign that you want to be sure you give them the information they need. Keep your answers concise. If an interviewer needs clarification, they will ask you for it. In some cases, this is preferred because it allows you and the interviewer to build a rapport.

One of my favorite examples of this was a young man I will call Sean, whom I interviewed for a coordinator role. He arrived for his interview fifteen minutes late. Although I was less than thrilled with the tardiness, he got points with me by calling to let me know he was running late. When I came to the lobby to greet him, he was dressed appropriately and shook my hand with confidence. As we walked back to the interview room, Sean said again how sorry he was that he was late and also added that should he get the job, his first priority was to move to the city. I appreciated that he wasn't overly apologetic but also didn't shy away from the situation. I liked that he took accountability for his actions. As we proceeded through the interview, Sean's responses were brief and to the point. He smiled and made eye contact with all of the members of the interview panel. He was warm, charming, eager, and intelligent. But so were most of the other candidates. I finally asked him the question, "Tell me about a time when you disagreed with a directive from a supervisor and how you resolved the situation." I was beginning to form my team, and I was still relatively new to the organization myself. It was a pretty cutthroat environment, and people disagreed just to disagree. You had to choose your battles very wisely. I wanted to effect change in the organization, but I also couldn't afford to alienate people. I needed to make sure that my team could stand up for themselves and our group without antagonizing anyone. Most of the candidates gave me an answer that indicated they would ultimately cave to whoever had the higher rank. Most admitted that they did this without even discussing the matter with anyone because, in their minds, that was the thing to do.

When I asked Sean the question, he was quiet for a moment. And then he said, "Would you like me to answer that for a major issue or a minor one?" That got my attention. I loved that he was asking me for clarification. I immediately said the minor one. This would allow me to see what Sean considered insignificant, which would be a good indication if he would be a cultural fit for the team. Also, if someone cares enough about something to bring it up as a point in an interview, chances are it is an issue that is important to them.

Sean proceeded to tell me a story about how he and a coworker had begun a practice they called Dress Up Friday. It was their way of rebelling against a too-casual dress code. But they also wanted to be role models for the disadvantaged youths they worked with and show them that they needed to take pride in their appearance. The leadership of his organization said nothing initially. However, he and his friend were eventually called into the office and told that their dressing up was seen as being nonconformist and was sending the wrong message to the staff. Other staff members felt Dress Up Friday was a comment on their casual dress and that Sean and his friend thought they were better than the rest of the team. Sean told his boss why they were doing Dress up Friday, and the manager acknowledged that several students were following in their footsteps and dressing a little better on Fridays. But he wanted the men to stop the practice because of how the rest of the staff was reacting. Sean asked if they could institute a policy for another day to dress up or have occasional dress-up days and have participants either donate money to a charity or earn credits they could use to wear jeans on a particular day. All his ideas were shot down. He left his manager's office, agreeing to wear casual clothes on Friday. His heart was warmed a bit when his student charges continued to come into their classes dressed up on Friday. Sean very wisely thought he needed to shift focus, so he and his colleague instituted Recognition Friday. Before classes started, each student had to recognize a fellow student for something, and the results were kept up on a board. Sean and his coworker always started the process, and they recognized colleagues as well as their students. Each student had to be acknowledged and had to acknowledge another student in return. The idea caught on like wildfire. It taught the students to always look for the good in each other, and Sean's manager absorbed the practice in team meetings. He even won an award for the idea. I hired him that day.

I needed a candidate who had formal education in adult learning theory as well as in learning design and development. Sean had no formal training in either. What Sean showed me was that he could stand up for himself and equally choose his battles. He showed that he wasn't easily dissuaded. He had found another way to meet his objective. In that small story, Sean had demonstrated his ability to be respectful, have integrity, negotiate, redirect, and win subtly -- all things that would serve him well in our environment and which I could not teach him. He did not have a learning and development background, but I could teach him that. Sean had successfully leveraged our interview to show me that although he did not have everything I was looking for in a candidate, he was an excellent fit for the organization and the team. He possessed qualities that were hard to teach to people—integrity, accountability, contentiousness, and the ability to influence without authority. To this day, I maintain he was one of the smartest hires I ever made.

## Second In-Person Interview

Congratulations, you have made it to the Question Round. In this round, you are most likely meeting with the person in charge—probably your future boss or your boss's boss. The good news is that the panel has determined that they can work with you and would like to. If you were a Miss America contestant, this would be where they ask you a question, and you let them know that the most important thing you want is world peace.

A few key points and objectives happen, or need to happen, at this phase. You must research the organization if you have not yet done that. LinkedIn and the internet are a boon for those looking for work because information is now at your fingertips, and everyone knows it. Do not squander that opportunity. I have found that no matter how intimidating the interviewer is to you, this is the phase where you will determine if you can work with this person. Bear in mind that as much as they are sizing you up, you need to size them up too.

## Here are a few tips to help you ace this part of the interview:

**Mind your body language.** Most communication cues are physical. Make sure that you smile and that you offer a firm handshake. Eye contact is crucial. And so is body language. If the interviewer fails to make eye contact or doesn't make small talk well beyond a brief sentence, chances are they don't want to hire you. You are a mandatory interview for them. There is a slight chance that you might be able to swing the conversation and interview in your favor, and you must try to do that in this situation, but don't be too disheartened if you are unable to turn the tides. In those cases, it was already set against you. The most you can do is to chalk the experience up to gaining practice and move on.

If you have gone through the usual small talk of getting there safely, weather, and maybe *How about those (fill in your sports team)?* then keep going. Size up your new boss. Look around their office. Are there awards to comment upon? Do you see a mounted diploma from your alma mater? Is there a book on the table that you have read? Always be looking for an entry point.

**Mind their body language.** Always look at the interviewer's body language. Are they ignoring you and reading your resume? They might be looking for something specific to ask you about, or this might be the first time they have seen your resume. Do they make eye contact with you, or are they looking at something else? Do they write anything down? Do they ask follow-up questions? What kind of impressions are you getting from them?

When I interviewed at the Dream Organization, my final interview round was with the Executive Vice President of Operations (EVP of Ops) to be followed by an interview with the person who would become my boss, the head of HR. It wasn't until I reflected later that I realized how differently both of those interviews had gone. The interview with the EVP of Ops was very intimidating. She was an accomplished and formidable woman. She grilled me relentlessly about my proudest accomplishment and how I persuaded others to see things my way. Halfway through the interview, she pulled out a strategic plan and a spreadsheet of figures and asked my opinion. I thought for sure she was testing me. I did well enough on the strategic plan, but point-blank told her figures were not my thing and asked if she wouldn't mind talking me through them so I could understand her priorities and what she felt was important to my role. She responded by closing the spreadsheet and thanking me for my time. I gulped and went on to talk with the next interview.

He was a nice man, although slightly distracted. His office was tiny and cramped. We sat at a table too big for the room, and he stared at my resume for most of the interview. He asked me questions like, *Name a project that didn't go well and why, and what would you do differently.* He made little eye contact and seemed pensive and thoughtful. We had a nice rapport, though, and I thought I could work with him.

A week after my interview, I was asked to speak with him again by phone to get some clarification. The questions he asked me were questions he had asked in the in-person interview. I wondered if I had not been clear enough in my responses. I was more than a little shocked but happy when a week later I was made an offer. And yes, you all know how that turned out for me. It is only now, in retrospect, that I have a clearer understanding of the interactions.

The EVP of Ops was indeed testing me. I later found out that she thought I had an extremely high executive presence, which she valued. What tipped the scale in my favor was that she appreciated my asking her for clarification on the spreadsheets. She liked that I had no problem admitting what I didn't know and then trying to learn more. The head of HR, however, was another story. He had phoned in my interview, and the follow-up call was an attempt to find an area he could use not to hire me. It didn't work. Had I done a better job of reflecting on the interview, I might have seen the red flags and not taken the role.

## Behavioral Interview Questions

It is not uncommon for recruiters to ask you behavior questions for the screening. Behavioral interview questions are structured to determine how an applicant might act in a given situation. Usually, you will be asked to answer based on prior experience. "Tell me about a time when you…" or "In the past have you done…" You want to make your responses brief and direct. I like to recommend four succinct sentences to respond to behavioral questions:

- Give the interviewer the situation.
- Let them know the problem or conflict.
- Tell them what you did to resolve it.
- Give the positive results of the action.

You may want to answer in more detail, but I would hold off on that. Allow them to think of follow-up questions. This is commonly called a conversation. If you apply this technique correctly, you will have piqued their curiosity about you, and they will want to know more. Always leave them wanting more.

## Follow Up Email or Card

People have powerful feelings about the follow-up email or thank-you card, and it is one of the biggest conundrums of interviewing. Being in HR, I have actually been in an office near a recruiter when they laughed at a handwritten thank-you they had received. I have also heard managers complain when they have not received thank-you notes. You should always thank someone for the time they have taken to speak with you. It might not appeal to them, but it lets them know the kind of person you are. And if this is not the kind of person you are, maybe this is a growth opportunity for you.

If you send a thank-you note, make sure you have the person's name and title correct. If they handed you their business card, that was the reason. Go ahead and send that note. Should it be email or handwritten? Email is more than acceptable in today's world, but often outside emails are blocked. If a recruiter has reached out to you via email, you should be OK, however. If you send something handwritten—which is my personal preference—don't send cute cards. Your standard thank-you note will do. Don't just say "thank you," either. This is a further opportunity to shine. Mention the interview without giving a play-by-play. Mention a key moment or information from the interview:

*Good Morning Ms. Jones,*

*Thank you again for the opportunity to speak with you and your team regarding the Learning Coordinator position. After learning more about the position from you and your team, I have no doubt that my prior experience running the LMS in my current role, as well as my recent MS Certification, will allow me to bring valuable skills to the position.*

*In addition, I was pleased to hear that your organization will be starting an Inclusion and Diversity initiative in September of this year. I am not new to this type of initiative as I have just joined the I & D council for my alumni association, and should I join your team would look forward to supporting the organization's I & D strategy.*

*Please reach out to me if I can answer any further questions. I look forward to hearing from you shortly.*

*Sincerely,*

*Robert (Rob) Sakamoto*

Your note should be quick and to the point. It should contain a thank-you and a further reason you would be an ideal candidate for the role. Be sure to mention a key factor or trait they are looking for in candidates and be sure to ask that question if they don't tell you. Be sure to include a reason that you can grow with the organization. Most companies don't want to hire someone who is just right for the role. They want employees who can grow a little with the company because this will justify not paying you at the ceiling of a role. It will give you a chance to grow into the role, and to learn the organization before you hopefully progress to another position within it.

Make sure you thank all the people who interviewed you, even those on any panels. I was once part of a panel, and the candidate we wanted to hire had forgotten to thank one of the members. She never forgave him even though he turned out to be an exemplary employee. Eventually, he became her boss and finally had it out with her. They were able to get past things, finally, but it soured what could have been an excellent working relationship for years.

Also, do not forget the recruiter. This is the person who pulled your resume out of the thousands (it can get that high, even with the help of filters) of other resumes in a pile and arranged for you to come in for an interview. Hiring managers are often way too busy and look to recruiters to be their gatekeepers and advisors. So do not forget the recruiter. Thanking the recruiter for their role in getting you to the job interview is a courtesy and a means of setting yourself up for future roles. Recruiters are people with whom you should always build strong, respectful relationships.

## Connecting on LinkedIn and Other Platforms

Here is another piece of advice I hope is helpful. LinkedIn benefits employers and employees alike. We use it to job hunt and network. We as interviewers can look up candidates. We can also look up our panels and interviewers. Personally, I like to see that an interviewee has looked me up because it shows they are willing to do a little homework. Even though this requires the same amount of effort as looking up a sports score, you do get points for trying. I have, however, been in a very awkward position on multiple occasions of a potential employee trying to connect with me or send me a message via LinkedIn before an interview. This is completely inappropriate. First of all, it puts me in a terrible position. If a recruiter or hiring manager reaches out to you to connect before an interview, it can cause the incorrect assumption that they are encouraging you. Do not do this. It is an unprofessional behavior and can cause a hiring manager or a company to rethink hiring you. If, however, the interview is over and you have received word that they have hired someone, even if it is not you, it is appropriate for you to reach out after a respectful stretch of time. Remember that you still want to leave a professional impression:

*Dear Mr. Barnes,*

*I enjoyed meeting you during the interview process for Company X. Although I wish things had ended differently, I am happy you found the right candidate for the Team Manager role.*

*I appreciate that you and your team will be implementing new software and wish you every success. After our meeting, I researched the XYZ process that you are using and would like to learn more about it. Can we connect on LinkedIn and stay in touch so that I can continue to develop my software skills?*

*Sincerely,*

*Malek Gupta*

Most of the time, I received an affirmative response. I have also done this with recruiters, and some of them have reached out to me even though I was not the preferred candidate. Some recruiters I have connected with contacted me to extend job offers when they moved to other companies. Some recruiters have reached out to me with offers from companies that hadn't wanted me for previous roles. I have also reached out to hiring managers asking them to act as a mentor or peer mentor for me. Seldom have I been rejected or met with apathy. We have to learn that we are all adults here and the networks we build are a reflection of us and what we do.

## Accepting an Offer

I hope you are reading this section because you have encountered the Holy Grail: a bona fide job offer. I may have mentioned that a recruiter once told me that I shouldn't even try to negotiate with her because I was out of work. Maybe because I had been out of work for a year or because my self-esteem had been deflated, I believed her. The mistake I made was that for the first time in my career, I didn't negotiate. I was afraid that I would lose the job offer I needed so badly if I did so. Regardless of your situation, you should negotiate, especially if you are offered something that is below your living expenses, or more importantly if you know is below your market value. Of course, the first thing is to know your market value. How do you do that? There are tons of websites such as Salary.com and glassdoor.com that will help you determine your worth. Market value is the term used to reflect what people in your field with your background and education can expect to be paid in the geographical area where you work. This will be and should be a range. Make sure you do your research on this even before you begin to look for work. Determine what your range is and stand firm. Keep in mind that there will be all kinds of things that fall into the range of compensation and that you might negotiate anything from time off to parking privileges. Employers include benefits like insurance, 401K match (some companies offer 4 percent to 6 percent), side benefits such as professional development, or tuition reimbursement. At one organization, I would have been able to attend work-related courses at a huge discount. Make sure you go through all of this with the recruiter and do not make your decision merely on base pay. When I accepted the offer, I forgot to factor in the cost of my long commute, and for the first time in my career, had the expense of toll roads.

Take everything into account. Bonuses. Stock options. Vacation days. Sick days. First, think about what you must have in take home pay to meet your usual (not unemployment) expenses. Then take into account the benefits they offer you. From there, you can tell whether or not they are meeting what you believe to be your fair market value and whether this total compensation will enable you to meet your expenses. Have reasonable expectations. If you want to work for a nonprofit and make the world a better place, I bow to you and your sense of moral justice—but I will share with you that the one time I worked for one, we took turns buying toilet paper for the office bathroom and there was no free coffee. You can imagine what the salaries were like. When I took a job with a large global company, they offered an array of benefits and a salary to match, but there were other reasons I selected that job, such as business class travel. You make the best choice for You, Inc.

Recruiters will tell you that they have no wiggle room on salary. I am always skeptical of that. They want to be able to get the best possible talent as cheaply as possible. But often, they are doing you a favor. If you accept a job with an organization at the ceiling or high range for your position, you will have nowhere to go as far as annual raises. You will top out at your range. And that means that you either need to move to another position in the company for a significant salary increase or get a promotion within your current role. Neither is unheard of; it is just good to know where you stand.

Also, bear in mind that you might not have wiggle room on salary, but you might on other things. I have been able to negotiate increased vacation days and a guarantee that I will be able to attend a certain number of conferences that I thought were crucial to my role, usually two to three a year. You can negotiate things like parking, too, which can cost $20 a day in a major city. You will have to carefully work everything out so that you know what your negotiables and non-negotiables are. For many people, things such as work-life balance are key. Do you need certain hours in order to come into work? Do you want to work from home a certain number of days a week? Keep all of those things in mind as you negotiate. Make sure your offer letter includes the things you negotiated. Although an offer letter is by no means a contract, at least you have it in writing.

Remember: Your state of unemployment does not define you. That is just your current circumstance. The company hiring you is not being magnanimous and hiring you just so you can have a job. They are hiring you for your skills, experience, and education, which is your cornerstone for negotiation. Remind them of that, nicely and professionally. Know your worth, and just as importantly, make sure that the company hiring you is also aware of it.

## Keep Interviewing, Even After the Offer

One of the reasons recruiting is such a tough job is that few organizations keep HR in the loop when they should. This mystifies me. HR is the department that protects an organization from risk, yet organizations treat HR as an afterthought. Rarely are they brought entirely into the loop for reorganizations or business pivots until well after decisions have been made. HR is expected to clean up rather than help plan. It should be the opposite, but leaders and hiring managers often look at HR as the group that gets in their way. Time and again, I have seen hiring managers extend offers to candidates who were not vetted through HR. I have also seen positions not funded well after candidates were interviewed and even after offers were extended. Keep interviewing until your first day of work. There are so many uncertainties in this world; it would be tragic for you to count on a role only to have it fall through at the last minute. And the truth is you will never know why. If this happens to you, I want you to have the safety net of other interviews and possibilities lined up.

## Settling

I hope each person who reads this has not only found something helpful in this book but is also getting an offer for their dream job. Or at the very least, a job that makes them happy and excited. We do not live in a completely just world, and do not always get what we want or deserve.

Here is where I will give you a piece of advice that every recruiter and many, many job candidates will scoff at, but keep in mind I am speaking from my perspective and experience. Often times, you will be told to only take a job at your level, which you truly want to do at an organization that meets your high standards. But that only works in a perfect world. I was in a situation where I took a job that was not exactly what I wanted. I took the job for practical and professional reasons, even though I was advised to hold out for a better fit for my background and career goals.

I got a job offer at the eleventh hour for a position not at the leadership level where I was used to working. I was facing several realities. Unemployment pay had run out, and I had borrowed money from my friends and maxed out my credit cards. My credit rating had plummeted from a sparkling Excellent rating to a tarnished Needs Work, balancing on that fine crossover line to Poor. It looked as if I wouldn't make my next mortgage payment, and I had a couple of late car payments on my record. I was eating ramen a couple of dinners a week and had already cashed in my change jar for gas money. I took that job. And it wasn't so bad, not bad at all. The pay met my monthly expenses. It was also with an organization I was very proud to work for. It allowed travel (pre-COVID) - I got to fly to Europe twice in business class. I got to work with an amazing group of professionals and even finally received a long-coveted certification. It is not a decision I wanted to make but I had to make, and once I reconciled with it, I was happy. I continued to look for work at a higher level, and when I was asked why I took a lower job, I replied honestly: "To keep my house." I then told people what I had accomplished in the new role and what I was really looking for, making sure I hit the high notes of what they were offering, and showed what I could do for them. Only you can make the exact and right choices for you and your family. I hope that this helps you see things from all angles and weigh them from a new perspective. I feel the stigma in taking a job at a lower level has been greatly reduced over the past year (2020) -- one of the few benefits of COVID-19. A role that does not quite meet someone's resume or expectations is commonly referred to as a bridge job, meaning it is a role you take in between the places you want to go. Sometimes you take a bridge job to learn new things. Other times you take it to receive a paycheck and benefits until you find a more suitable role. If you need to take a job, and it meets the majority of your needs, take the job.

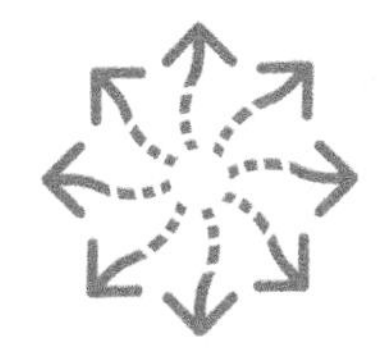

# 9
# A MESSAGE FOR RECRUITING

I come from HR and know that it is not an easy field. Employees and candidates want you to be their best friend, and sometimes, savior, and hiring managers want you to be a combination of a mind reader and magician. Too often, HR is asked to be the empathetic branch of an organization. I feel this is wrong. Twenty years of leading Talent Management has taught me that being the humanistic and empathetic branch of an organization is the job of leaders, not HR. HR's role in an organization is to mitigate risk.

Recruiting has a more significant role than people realize. Their role is to find and recruit top talent for an organization. Too often, an organization does not give recruiting enough training, time, and resources to do so. Often, recruiting is forced to be reactionary: *OMG, Bob just got promoted, so we need to find a new head of Marketing, now!* So if Bob in Marketing moves to Communications, who internally can take his role, and what are the qualities we would need from someone we hired outside the organization? It doesn't help recruiters that candidates apply for any job where they feel remotely qualified because it is easy to do and because of the hope that someone will notice them. We have all done it; admit that you have. Please stop. Thanks to the electronic age and sites such as LinkedIn and Indeed, we now know what jobs are available at which companies faster than ever and have the ease of uploading a file resume and hitting send to apply. What, Facebook needs a new VP of Communications? Sure, I ran the college newspaper; I'll apply for that. Pinterest needs a new Director of Learning? I'll apply; after all, I am completely qualified. But no, I have no intention of living in San Francisco. It's just fun to dream. Do the recruiters and other candidates a favor and don't apply to everything. We fill up recruiters' inboxes and place good, qualified candidates in a sea of resume litter just because we can. Stop it. Step away from the laptop. Apply only for the jobs that you truly desire and for which you are reasonably qualified.

My recent experience being out of work and interacting with several recruiting teams through multiple levels of interviews leads me to think there is room for improvement in the process. It does not pain me in the slightest to say this because I feel this way about any job: If you are not willing to complete all of the functions of your job to your utmost ability in a professional manner and at a high standard, you shouldn't be doing that job. Yes, there are functions of all of our jobs that we do not like, but that doesn't mean we get to avoid them or do them poorly. I feel the same about recruiting. As I said, recruiting is not always the easiest job. If you genuinely do not want to help your organization, find the most talented people for each position, and do not want to treat them with the utmost courtesy and professionalism, then don't do the job.

This is not only the flaw of recruiters but also the fault of their employers and organizations. All too often, recruiters are held accountable for the number of vacant positions they can fill and how quickly they can do it, not for the people's quality and their fit into the organization.

In some unfortunate cases, it is a job that requires no finesse. No real skill. It has become a transactional and not a strategic role.

I might not know the difference if it hadn't been for one of the best recruiters I have ever met, a woman who changed my life. In 2006 I was working a job that was not right for me. I had been trying to get back into HR to no avail and seriously pondered a complete career change. I continued to work in a place I didn't like while my frustration grew. I had had so many near misses with jobs that it was border lining on pathetic. I had finally scored an interview with a major healthcare company. I went to the interview and hit it off with the recruiter immediately. We talked about Aaron Sorkin films and traded anecdotes about our line of work. Margaret, the recruiter, was a lovely woman with a gleam in her eye. In the interview, I asked why she had called me in. She explained that the company, Magellan, had just come out of a hiring freeze, and she was new to the organization. She literally found my resume on her desk her first day and then realized there was a job opening for which I was qualified. I left her office feeling hopeful. Later that week, she called to tell me that my interview with her had made her rethink the job and wanted to do a phone follow-up. I complied, ever hopeful. A week later, she told me that, in retrospect, I wasn't a good fit for the job. I thanked her for letting me know. I recall being disappointed but rather pleased that I had somehow helped her refigure the job. A couple of weeks later, she called to tell me there was another role available, and she thought I would be an excellent fit. I went through the interview process and knew from the way the hiring manager spoke with me that I would not get the role. Sure enough, Margaret called me back within a few days to confirm my suspicion. I appreciated her always calling me back and treating me like I was a valued person.

A year later, I still hadn't changed jobs and had just given up. One day, I got home, and there was a message on my answering machine: "Hello Sabina, this is Margaret from Magellan. Do you remember me? I remember you, and I have a job available that I think you would be perfect for. Give me a call as soon as you can." Trust me, this sort of thing does not happen very often in the world of job seeking, and it should.

I called Margaret the next day. She explained that the job was in Learning and Development. I explained that was not my area of HR. Confidently she said, "Trust me, you are perfect for this job." I went in the next day to interview with the VP of Learning. I went on later that week to meet with two other people from the department. A quick background check and I not only had a new job but also a new career. Margaret was right, Learning and Development was the path for me. That is how it should be. And it seldom is.

## Contacting people

Recruiters, keep a few things in mind when you initially reach out to people. First, you are taking up their time and yours. Both are valuable. Only contact someone if you think they are a good fit for the role and the organization. Not if you think they might be. Or not if you believe that with some coaching, they might be. Not if the hiring manager really, really, really wants you to call his wife's best friend's kid. Be firm about this. Otherwise, you are wasting your time and giving false hope.

The time you take to reach out to the prospective candidate is time you might be missing out on the ideal one. From a humanistic perspective, if you reach out to someone looking for work, you set off a spark of hope in them. It is just human nature. If you happen to reach out to someone who has been out of work for a while, the spark is bigger and it ignites something in them. They are already checking out you and your organization on LinkedIn. They are already calculating the commute to your location. They are beginning their pitch to you. They are already planning what it would be like to work for you and come into the office each day. It is a given. It's what people do.

So be careful and be gentle when you light that spark. Treat everyone with kindness and professionalism. You represent your organization. If you reach out to that one person who will make a difference and you are less than professional, you could be losing the best candidate you have ever encountered.

## Ghosting

In early 2020, there was a huge debate on LinkedIn about ghosting, the practice of ending contact without explanation. A few recruiters chimed in to justify the practice, saying that the ease of using technology to apply meant there were too many candidates to reach out to. That, I completely understand. It would not be financially astute or physically possible to reach out to everyone who submits a resume via the internet. But that is not what we who cast the ghosting stone mean. We mean that when you have contacted us (a candidate)—be it for an interview or a phone screen—and we have spoken to you, a person, you need to reach back out to us. One recruiter mentioned that the hiring manager doesn't always let recruiting know the decision. And you let that happen? Shame on you and your manager.

I do not care if it sounds like I am a thousand years old; I do not like nor understand the concept of ghosting. Any job hunter will tell you that they experience it every day. To the job seeker, I know that you send out dozens of resumes a week and get an automated reply for a fair number of them. That is perfectly acceptable in our digital world.

But once direct contact is made, in my mind, it sets up a rapport and an obligation. The rule in my book is "direct communication for direct communication." For example, if I receive an email and I respond, I expect at least an email in return. If someone calls me, even if it is for a phone screen, I expect at least an email back letting me know that either I am going on to the next round or that they have decided not to move forward with me. I can live with that. Once we get to the interview stage and beyond, I expect to be treated with an appropriate amount of professionalism.

I was interviewing for a job with a well-known international investment house for two months. I had multiple phone screens and interviews. I went into D.C. for two separate all-day interviews. I never heard back from the organization. I assume I didn't get the job. Recruiters will counter with how overworked they are or that giving bad news is so hard. Telling me I didn't get the job is disappointing to me. However, not hiring me if I am not a good fit is something of a favor. Treating me as if I am inconsequential in the process? That is plain rude.

Think back to my Margaret story. What if she had ghosted me in 2006 and then tried to call me in 2007? Would I have gone in for an interview? I probably would not have returned her call. And that would have been unfortunate for so many reasons. I had a very successful tenure at Magellan. I learned a tremendous amount about talent management and found a whole new career. Had I been ghosted, who knows where I would be today? In addition, I gave a lot to Magellan. I designed a supervisor orientation that was in use for over a decade. I pioneered webcasting and podcasting for learning at the organization. In 2008 when the recession hit, I was one of the few people still allowed to travel. I became the unofficial ambassador for corporate learning throughout the organization. A supervisor wrote in my review that it was astounding that I was able to reach across the aisles to connect with people. I pioneered a type of training for managers, teaching them how to manage teams working remotely. I understand the training program was dusted off to be used during the pandemic. None of this would have happened if Margaret had ghosted me. She was and is a unicorn.

I am not a disgruntled job seeker. I do not hold the recruiters solely responsible for this situation. I largely blame the companies for which they work. Companies pay millions of dollars for computer systems. They spend months coming up with a campaign to make their organization The Best Place to Work. They give executives huge bonuses. But I will never understand why they are not committed to having a decent recruiting department to help them hire top talent. It breaks your heart. If you do not put dollars, resources, and top-notch policies into the team that hires the people who run your machine, how on earth do you expect to have the people you want and need working for your organization? And if you read this and you answer that you already invest in that, shame on you. You have just told me that you do not invest because anyone with a top-notch proactive leadership team who truly cares and wants to continue that curve would reply, *Tell me more. I want to improve things.*

## Let me use the bathroom, please

Let's talk about the interview process itself. If you, the recruiter, have brought someone in to be interviewed, please think about how this will go best for everyone involved. In most cases, organizations try to be expeditious, and they set up panel or round-robin interviews for a day. This way, everyone only has to block a single day off their calendar, and they get things done. Please think this through, and account for the variables. Account for the fact that someone—be it a hiring manager, an interviewer, or me—will be running late. Think about whether an interview is going well and there are clarifying questions. Think about the fact that someone will have to use the restroom—probably me or any other candidate who has traveled to your location and probably got there early and probably hung out at the local coffee place for a half-hour before their interview.

One of the most exhausting interviews I ever had was with a company in southern Maryland. An executive search firm set it up, and I initially spoke with the head of HR. He had me come back to meet the rest of the team and leadership. I was scheduled for a full day of interviews, for which the search firm sent me a schedule. It was a long, tiring day.

- 9 a.m. Bill Smith, Recruiting
- 10 a.m. Bob Jones, Marketing
- 11 a.m. Mary Pringle, Communications
- 12-12:45 p.m. Lunch with the team
- 1 p.m. Brett James, CEO
- 2 p.m. Follow up with Harry in HR

I hope you see what I see: No bathroom break. Lunch with the team is great, but who can eat and talk at the same time? This is why I have a major issue with lunch interviews. So here I was with a long drive to get to the location. I timed it, so I arrived with enough time to freshen up before my interviews, but security informed me that to use the bathroom, my host had to sign me in. Harry waited until the last minute to greet me, leaving me no time to use a facility. It was a very long day. Finally, I had the opportunity to use the restroom right before our follow-up, four hours after I had entered the building. I realized if I had gotten that job, that is what my days would have been like.

Remember to treat people professionally and to schedule breaks and time for food and restrooms. This isn't the hardest thing to figure out. Think about this as if you were the one being interviewed. I bet you'd want to use the bathroom and even eat something at lunch.

## How you treat me will reflect on your organization

Back in college, I used to work for a very nice hotel. It was my main training ground for how to do a job well. It was indeed training by fire, and one thing stuck out to me. One kind executive at the hotel came downstairs (executives lived in the hotel as we were opening for business), and she complimented me on how I answered the phone. She said I had a pleasant, polite manner but that I also sounded warm and friendly. She said that was how she wanted people to think of the hotel. "Remember, you are most people's first impression of the hotel," she said. "Make sure it is always a good one." That message has stayed with me for my entire career. Whoever I work for, I realize I represent the organization. Even if you know a company by name and reputation, the first human contact with anyone from an organization will always be your main impression of a company. As the saying goes, you only have one chance to make a first impression.

Make sure emails are polite but to the point and spelled correctly. Answer within 48 hours, although 24 is better. Recruiters often give the impression that they think applicants need the job more than the company needs the candidate. I will never understand this. I have been at companies where too often, we have lost well-qualified candidates because someone else moved faster. I worked for an IP concern, and we were trying to hire someone as a senior vice president for Customer Success. A vice president recommended someone who she had worked with in the past. The candidate was quickly ushered in for interviews with key executives, and everyone agreed that we should hire him. One board member wanted to wait until after the holidays. The VP who recommended the candidate pushed back to no avail. We waited three weeks to extend an offer. The candidate politely responded that they had taken a job with Amazon two and a half weeks before. When asked why they didn't let us know, he rightly replied, "When I didn't hear back from you, I assumed you weren't interested in me anymore." You are always in competition for top talent. Moving quickly is essential.

## Tell me the important things I need to know

Six weeks after I sent my resume to a global corporation, I was contacted for a phone screen. A week later, they called back to schedule onsite interviews. Interviews were scheduled for almost a full month later, partly because of a holiday and to accommodate some of the people's travel schedules. I appreciated that the interviewer gave me a reasonable expectation. I met with everyone early in the month. The onsite interviews went quite well. But there were also cracks. I was given nebulous instructions about how to come into the building. The front of the building faced a busy highway and parking was in the rear. It was hard to figure out how to get to the front of the building from the back without going in. Also, it had snowed that day. Luckily, I allowed plenty of time to drive the hour from my home. When I got to the security desk, the admin who came to greet me looked very annoyed. She explained that she had a lot to do that day and taking care of me was inconvenient.

Great. Not only that, but she sent me to a small conference room and said that most of my interviews would be held via video conference. I drove through a blizzard for this? One of the interviewers, who ironically became a good colleague, actually told me in the video conference that he only lived twenty minutes away but didn't feel like driving to the office in the snow. Another future coworker told me that she just didn't want to come in that day. The interview was scheduled over the course of the day, and no one had thought to either make lunch arrangements for me or forewarn me that I needed to take care of my meal. The hiring manager gamely ate lunch with me. It was extremely awkward as we tried to make conversation while eating food that came out of the refrigerated catering kiosk in the building. I should have seen these early red flags, but I was impressed that the head of the department spent an hour and a half with me. He made me want to work for the company. On balance, the positives of the job and the chance of working for a global organization outweighed my negative interview experience. I left feeling good about my chances of getting the job.

A month went by without a word from the company. I was surprised, but I moved on. I interviewed at other organizations. Then out of the blue, they called four weeks later to ask if I was still interested in the job. Since I had not settled with anyone else, I said "yes." The recruiter then requested that I come back to the company to interview with one more person. I almost said "no," but I went. After that final interview, the manager I liked came back into the room. He told me that the original hiring manager was leaving her role, and he wanted me to know since they were extending me an offer.

Two more weeks went by without an offer. I finally had to track the recruiter down. She said her husband was ill, but she would send me something soon. Another two weeks went by. I continued to interview and send out resumes. She promised to send me something soon. Finally, after two more weeks, I got the offer letter. The recruiter informed me that the company did not allow people to start each week, and I was dependent upon their orientation schedule for my start date. That would have been almost six months from my initial application. They were able to squeeze me into the orientation earlier, but I always felt like I was labeled a complainer for insisting upon starting as soon as possible. I was as put off with the lack of communication from the organization as I was with the lengthy time it took me to get from application to the first day of work. Had someone from the company been in good contact with me along the way, I would have understood the delays. It would have given me a better feeling toward the company. It would have made me feel valued.

If you have a good and streamlined communication process among hiring managers, recruiters, HR, etc., the hiring process should be efficient and quick. Hold people accountable for making sure that you quickly and adequately hire new employees. The glacial pace of the hiring process at most organizations and the complete lack of communication with candidates never ceases to amaze me. Worse, it causes organizations to lose solid and even great candidates. As a candidate, it feels awful.

## Yes, I am unemployed, and I am still going to negotiate -- Part II

Another issue I cannot fathom is the absolute inability or unwillingness of recruiters to negotiate salary. The metric for most organizations is to keep hiring costs and salaries as low as possible. This never makes sense to me. Especially when the same organizations then complain about lack of talent or their inability to find top talent. You get what you pay for. Most organizations are reactive, not strategic, about salaries and their ranges. When recruiters call, they do not take into account the applicant and their experience. Instead, they are focused on the job they are trying to fill and its parameters. I often applied for positions I was overqualified for. The longer I was unemployed, the more desperate I became. Remember I told you that we all applied to jobs that we are not necessarily qualified for? That swings both ways as we, in desperation, apply for jobs for which we are over-and-under-qualified. But recruiters were by no means obligated to call me back. One company, unsolicited, called me for a learning specialist role, a job I had eons ago. They said they wanted someone who could take over the department and make it into something. So far, so good. It was a Fortune 500 company and a staff of 12. The job description, title, and pay did not match the expectations for the role. Finally, the recruiter and I had talked about what I wanted for compensation. I gave her my floor, realizing it was way above her ceiling. She refused to budge, saying, "I am not sure why you think you can call the shots. You're unemployed." I call the shots because I am talented and experienced, and I know my worth.

You should always negotiate with top talent. If you buy a Smart car, you get a Smart car—small, kind of dependable, gets you where you need to go. If you want to get there with speed and efficiency, some style and dependability, you must aim higher and be prepared to pay for it. Otherwise, you get what you pay for.

## Make sure you know what the hiring manager wants

One of the best job experiences I ever had was when I worked for a global IP company. Even though we had a recruiting office, the task of writing job descriptions often fell first to the hiring manager and then to the HR Business Partner (HRBP). I had been working on a project where I was determining the necessary skills and competencies for a department, and one of the roles that needed a job description redo was in that department. The HRBP of the group had asked for my input on the job description. I was floored and pleased. Between the two of us, we were able to take the hiring manager's job description, refine it and then add the skills and needs I had identified as essential to job success. She and I happily repeated that pattern whenever a new job occurred in her work area. We had a blast doing it, often bringing hiring managers into the process. Better yet, we were able to hire skilled talent that had staying power within the company and more than met the hiring managers' expectations. All because we knew what they were looking for. These conversations were not always easy. Often we had to coax information from hiring managers in an intense and rigorous process. Pinning them down to time commitments was not always easy. But in the end, our approach was efficient and effective.

Recruiters, make sure you know exactly what the hiring manager is looking for in candidates, and know their work area. Act as a consultant. Recruiters see the hiring trends, and worse, the termination trends in their organization, more and better than anyone else. Please act like the experts you are.

## A final word to candidates

I hold job candidates just as accountable for their actions and practices as I would hold recruiters accountable. I believe it is possible to set expectations and boundaries with recruiters as far as what you are looking for in a job and how you want to be treated. Ultimately, it is your choice.

Do not let desperation be your only influencer. Before you accept a job offer, ask yourself this question: If you were still in your old job, would you take the one being offered to you? If the answer is "yes," then take it. If the answer is "no," then you either need to take the job, knowing it was your choice to accept it (and maybe like me, you had good reasons), or you need to move on. I am not going to tell you not to settle. I am telling you to make decisions with a clear head and understand all you are getting into. If an organization does not have a good recruiting and interview process, do not assume that this is the only part of the organization that needs work and make decisions accordingly. Remember, you always have a choice. This is one choice that you might have to live with for a while.

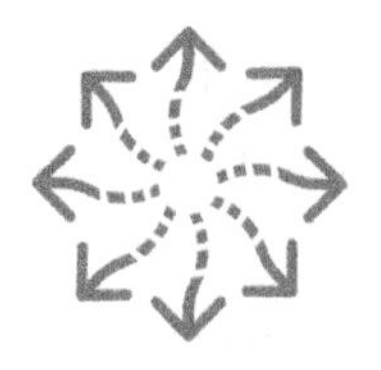

# 10

# BEFORE RETURNING TO WORK

While everyone's unemployment experience will be different, the same can also be said for your back-to-work experience. I hope you have landed in a role that excites and invigorates you. And let us be honest, sometimes you have to take a role because you have to be practical. I have been very disappointed by the know-it-all recruiters and executive search firms who have told me that you should never take a job below your level or one that you don't love. One of them even had the temerity to say to me, "Well, I can talk, as I am living in a house that's paid for. You're just unlucky." Thank you, I look forward to your self-esteem YouTube videos. But seriously, you have landed a job for whatever reason, and you should be pleased; you should feel elated. Here are a few things to do before and after your first day back to work.

Even if you have been out of work for only a brief time, you will soon have an income coming in and you have added to your purpose and passion. For that, you should revel in the accomplishment. I hope you set aside something for a celebration or acknowledgment of your achievement, as I suggested.

Upon receiving a firm job offer, my first action was to email and text the friends who stood by me. I was so happy to tell them that their support for me mattered so much and to thank them. It also helped me talk out a few things as the role I took was not everything I wanted it to be. But through great friends who provided greater words of wisdom, I was able to see that I was letting my fear of returning to work get the best of me. By talking through the situation, I was able to see all the wonderful benefits of my new job (beyond the pay and insurance) and that this was a fantastic opportunity for me. I had set out to obtain a head of learning role in a global organization with a social conscience that would also allow me to travel. That is exactly what I accomplished. I had a great job in a great organization with a good paycheck and some amazing perks. Spoiler alert, I spent a month visiting our sites in Europe, and I loved it. An unforeseen bonus was that for the first time in my career, I got to work with a large group of peers in my field. The learning community at the company ended up being one of the most rewarding perks of my career.

Another reason to share and celebrate your accomplishment is that the act of celebration changes you psychologically. If you have been unemployed, you have experienced everything from depression to fear. Worse, if you have been on multiple interviews, you have experienced a series of ups and downs emotionally. It is expected that when we begin to interview for a job, we begin to feel hope. We begin to see our world as it might be. We become excited. It is part of human nature that we begin to see the future through that lens. Bluntly put, on a good day, hope can run circles around depression. As we continue to act and behave with hope, the idea of possible can turn to probable. In this phase, we are no longer exuberant and excited; we become confident and assured.

It is almost seductive. *Maybe* somehow turns to *Yes* before we can stop it because we want or need what we believe will happen to become real.

If the object of our hope slips through our fingers, we coast through disappointment, and physics takes over: The higher we reach, the lower we fall. Our depression and anxiety become even deeper, and the prospect of starting all over again becomes almost unbearable until hope crooks her index finger and beckons us once more. This is one of the reasons I urge you to invest but not to attach. It is not easy to do.

If you have been on the job hunt for some time, chances are you have gone through and been burned by this cycle more than once. I have described my own ins and outs and ups and downs while looking for work. I would not wish it on my worst enemy. If you are like me, you stopped telling your friends about interviews because you just did not want to have to tell them that it didn't happen. Again. You began to wonder what was wrong with you and why you are failing. The last thing you want to do is have to hear your friends echo the same thoughts that you barely admit to yourself.

It is not abnormal to get a job offer and still feel anxious and uneasy despite getting what you wanted- a job. You may experience many things when the offer happens. After years toiling in an awful job for a company that seemed to have weekly layoffs, I finally got a job in my chosen field after what seemed like an eternity of trying. A very dear friend, Kathleen, took me to dinner to celebrate and gave me what has now become my standard gift to friends who get new jobs: A lovely bag filled with all the things a young female executive would need for her desk. It was so thoughtful and sweet. I still recall everything being pink and black. I assumed Kathleen thought the combination was both feminine and intimidating. I still have a few of the pens she gave me and one of the notebooks. What I recall the most was her card. Besides wishing me well and telling me that she knew all along I could do it, it said, "I know you think this isn't real, but it is, and it isn't going away." I still have that card because I loved the thought, but more than, that I could never figure out how Kathleen had bored into my brain and soul to know precisely what I was thinking and feeling. Whenever I felt anxiety in the first few weeks of that job, I looked at that card and let the message wash over me.

Kathleen had hit the nail on the head. She knew that I had been through the ups and downs of interviews and disappointments, and she knew that even the signed offer letter wouldn't quite seem real. Note that this is not the same as imposter syndrome, the feeling that you really do not deserve your job and that sooner or later, someone will figure that out. You know you can do the job because you did it somewhere else. You know you have the skillset. You are just not used to hope and possibility turning into reality. You are waiting for that far more familiar feeling of depression, anxiety, and loss. You probably experienced the roller coaster with every resume you sent out, with every phone screen you took, and with every interview you attended. You also might be feeling the simple effects of change. You are used to being at home. You have a routine that you are now attached to if you did it successfully. I loved the daily routine I developed for myself. I looked forward to journaling, meditation, and self-help books. I resented that going back to work, no matter how essential, would be a massive change for me.

At the beginning of this book, I mentioned how losing your job causes change. Now that you have a new job, you will experience a different change as you return to work. It is not that people dislike change. They may disagree with it, but that is not necessarily where they have the complaint. It is the transition to change that people dislike.

One of my favorite TV shows is *Love It or List It.* On the show, the two hosts compete to either find the family a dream home or change their existing home to suit the family, and the family must decide to Love it or List It. Resoundingly, most families choose to stay in their current homes, even if they don't get all the renovations they want, no matter how perfect the "new" property is for them. I am convinced that one of the reasons that people choose to stay is because someone has done all the hard work for them. What people hate about change is not the change itself but the work they will have to do to get there. Starting a new job is like that. On the show, the hard work is done for the family, and they can reap the rewards. Life is not like that. The longer you have been unemployed, the harder it will be to get back into the flow of returning to work. Here are some things to do to help you get on track.

## Bask, share, and celebrate!

These are two different activities. First, I recommend basking in the moment by yourself. Congratulations! You just did something remarkable: you bounced back. If you want to open that nice bottle of wine friends brought back from Napa, please do so. If you want to go for a five-mile run while you still have time to exercise, please do so. If you want to munch on that Snickers bar that you hid in the back of your refrigerator, please do so. Whatever form your celebration takes, please enjoy it and revel in it. This is your moment. You, Inc.'s stock is at an all-time high.

Now that you have patted yourself on the back, it is time to brag a little. Hopefully, if you are like me, you have had some amazing friends/family who have been cheering you all the way. Share this accomplishment with them. It doesn't have to be the same day, but it should be soon. These are the people who root for you when you were down. Who let you cry on their shoulders. Who prayed for you. Let. Them. Know. You. Won!!!

I did not wait long to text or email my friends. Some I even called. I think I heard the collective sigh of relief of everyone I knew. My friends were happy for me. They were relieved that I found the light at the end of the tunnel. I still have the voicemail from my mentor, and the joy in her voice still gives me pleasure. Anytime I have a terrible day, I replay it, so I remember that someone had faith in me and that positive change just around the corner. You decide how and when you want to let everyone know. Some you will email, some you will text, some you will call, and some folks deserve to be told in person. Your partner, your children, those who supported you the most, and who depend on you—this is a winning moment for everyone.

Now that you have told everyone, it is time to *really* celebrate. A celebration, especially a public and shared one, kicks off the change and helps you develop the new mindset of someone who goes to work every day. It informs your friends and family that you are starting on a new journey and they should support you. It also lets you know that you have that support as you mentally begin the journey of returning to work. A celebration—really, shouldn't it be a series of celebrations?—is a way to say goodbye to your life of being unemployed. It is a way to acknowledge that you have come through a challenging time and triumphed. You are starting to shrug off those feelings of rejection, depression, and anxiety and exchanging them for ones of excitement and possibility. We use celebrations as a way to bond and transition through change. Pick your celebration(s) carefully. Make it mean something.

Celebrating does not have to cost a lot of money. Money might be tight by the time you find work. There is no shame in this. For me, telling my friends about my new job was a celebration in itself. I chose to take a day to focus on the routine I had put in place, knowing that once I started work, most of it would be difficult to maintain. By the time I got a job, I had been unemployed for almost a year. Luckily, I found an old gift card, and one by one, I met with my friends for a celebratory lunch. Half the time when I told the wait staff what we were celebrating, they gave us free desserts and cocktails. Everyone loves to help you celebrate.

I would also suggest you find something deeply symbolic to do in order to celebrate. Something that doesn't cost money but will help you say goodbye to this challenging phase of your life. Think of it as a means of closing one chapter and opening the next. Earlier I discussed the importance of rituals, which help us to do things mindfully and intentionally. If you find that idea awkward, think of doing something as a symbolic gesture. I picked a day and went to the grocery store and used up the last dollar amount on my Independence/SNAP card. I had initially hoped to use it to make a donation at the store to the local food pantry, but you cannot use your card for that. I took my cart and bought lots of non-perishable items and donated them to the local shelter. For me, it was a way to give back and symbolized that I was going back to a way of life where I could help others. I have known people who burn all the check stubs from their unemployment compensation. I have known others who celebrated by deleting all the rejection notices from their email accounts. (That one is particularly satisfying.) You will figure out what your ritual should be. Just make sure you follow through. You will be pleasantly surprised at the satisfaction you feel.

## Close Out Old Business

The difference between being out of work for some time and going from one job to a new one is *time*. If you already have a job, most companies understand that you need to give adequate notice when you leave to end projects, train your replacement, etc. In the U.S., there is no law about this. It is more or less a mark of professionalism. Some countries in Europe have strict regulations about this. In countries such as Sweden, employees can take up to a year to transition from one job to the next. In the United Kingdom, employees usually have a contract with their employer that states how much notice they have to give, and new employers are perfectly understanding about it. Not in the U.S. Sometimes when you give notice for a job, the response from your current company is that you no longer have to worry about coming in and to go home for the remainder of your time. I have gotten that one. Usually, it is because they are afraid of what you will do or say to other employees, or they want to prevent you from taking documents, secrets, etc. Although you can be fired in the U.S. for cause, you cannot be fired for giving notice on a job. However, it is a very different situation when you are going from being unemployed to going back to work. If you are unemployed, your new company may want to take advantage of the fact that you do not have to give two weeks' notice and ask you to start right away. And it is very tempting. You might jump at the chance for a host of reasons: wanting to make a good impression, wanting to be out of the house, wanting to be productive, or wanting to start receiving a paycheck as soon as possible. Think before you make that decision. Take a few minutes and think about the life you have structured while out of work.

Just as you had to complete several tasks as you entered employment, you must alter your daily structure again to adapt to going back to work. While unemployed, you have worked very hard to build your resilience. Staying strategic and taking care of yourself and your family holistically is a huge part of your newfound strength. Perhaps you were doing things while unemployed that touched the lives of others. Maybe you had started to drop the kids off at school, and now, with a new job, this will be impossible. Talk to your children and spouse about this and come up with another activity to take its place so that you still have quality family time. If you have ongoing things, such as mentoring or volunteer work think about how your newly won employment will impact that. I had become a more active volunteer at my college and decided I did not want to stop, so I adjusted what I did and the hours when I did it. I had also begun taking classes at the local community college, which I reluctantly chose to shelve while I adjusted to my new job. Take the time to reflect upon the different areas of your life to see how they will change when you return to working. Be sure to make alternate plans where you must *before* you take on the responsibilities of a new job.

You may have taken a part-time job, a temporary full-time job, or are actively engaged in the gig economy. Be professional if you give notice: Do not burn bridges and be aware that karma is always watching. Maybe you want to continue your alternative source of income to help you get back on your feet. Just think all these things through and know that you will have to decide quickly.

**Benefits.** If you have been using your unemployment benefits (and why shouldn't you?), you must make sure that you let the benefits providers know that you have found a job. Some benefits offices/agencies to notify include:

**Health Insurance.** Employers start health insurance at different times for new employees. In most cases, you no longer have to wait to get past the 90-day probationary period. I was fortunate in that my new company started its employee benefits on Day One. That is almost unheard of. Find out when your new employer begins benefits for new employees and have the information ready to tell your current insurance provider, even if you are on Medicaid. Do not officially stop your current insurance benefits until the new ones take effect. Just be ready for it. Mark the day on your calendar or phone so you have your new insurance cards ready and have confirmed providers before you cut ties from the old one.

If you chose to buy your own insurance when you were unemployed, you could keep it. If you went on your partner's insurance, you do not have to be removed from it unless you wish. It is best to sit down with all your plan options and a list of crucial medical needs so you can make the right decisions. For example, while I was out of work, one of my doctors suggested exploratory surgery. This doctor did not take Medicaid, and since the surgery was only exploratory, I postponed it. However, as soon as I received a job offer and knew the insurance providers, I checked to ensure my doctor took one of the plans. I scheduled the surgery immediately. Keep in mind that you will be tied to any decision you make until the end of the calendar year.

**Unemployment Pay.** You may have been lucky enough to have gained employment before your benefit ended. Do not forget to inform your state unemployment office that you now have a paying job. In most cases, you will continue to get unemployment until your first paycheck, but the policy and the process for this vary from state to state. Make sure you take care of these steps now to know what the process is and the timeline. Ending benefits should be simple enough to do online or over the phone. Continuing benefits after you have a job can be a nightmare to resolve. Additionally, you do not want to be the person who kept benefits they did not need. Or deserve.

**Independence Card Benefits.** If you are receiving SNAP benefits that you no longer need, let your state organization know. In my state, Maryland, benefits were provided electronically to a debit card on the first of each month. When I accepted my new job, I didn't know I would have a start date early in the month, so I had already received my benefits by the time I started my new job. Because I was single and highly frugal, I had the new month's benefits and the money from the prior month on my card—a total of about $600. My new job was going to send me on a business trip immediately, so I had plenty of time before I needed to buy groceries, and I still had a well-stocked pantry. I repeatedly called the state to try to return my unused benefits, to no avail. Finally, a friendly but world-weary state employee told me that in her recollection, I was asking for something that no one had ever done before. She advised me to just have a dinner party to celebrate my new job. Instead, I went on that massive supermarket spending spree and donated proceeds to the local shelter. It was probably one of the best things I have ever done in my life.

## Getting Ready for Returning to Work

Remember getting ready for that first day of school (back when kids went to school)? You made sure you had all your school supplies ready, you might have gotten a new haircut, brand-new clothes, and you might have packed lunch the night before? Going back to work is very much like that. Going back to work combines the excitement of the new with the anticipation of the unknown. Just as you did when you were a kid, as you go back to work, take care of the things you can control, and hope that gives you enough solace to face the things you cannot.

**Appearances Matter**. I hope you squirreled away some cash to bankroll yourself to look picture perfect for the interview process. But, if your process took significant time, you might have to rebook all those appointments to make sure you look your best for that security ID photo that will follow you for what you hope will be a nice, long tenure at your new gig. Do that as soon as possible, as well as you can afford to do.

Let's talk about clothes. Ensure you have enough clean and ready clothes to get you through the first two weeks of work. I would err on being a little dressier and more conservative in the first few days. After COVID-19, we are even more relaxed in how we come to work, but I also maintain that you cannot come back from being too casual at work, but you can always lighten up your appearance to fit in. Take the story of a VP I met in a leadership development class for a major insurance company. The company prided itself in promoting from within and it was not unheard of for admins to one day be managers and managers going on to be VPs. This VP had started as a claims adjuster (their first-ever job) and worked his way up. On his first day, being told the dress code was casual and being fresh out of high school, he came in wearing jeans (which were allowed) and a tie-dyed Grateful Dead T-shirt (which was not). They let him work through the rest of his first day in August while wearing a sweater he happened to have in his car. He told me that someone brings up this story to him at least once a year. Despite all his success, he will always be known as the VP Who Wore Tie-Dye. Do not let that be you.

**Car and Transportation.** You have probably had to cut back on spending and may not have kept up with the maintenance and appearance of your car. But you only get one chance to make a first impression. Be sure your car is reliable and clean. If you think you can spare the expense, take your car to the mechanic for a once-over or at the very least a place that replaces all your fluids and checks the tire pressure. The last thing you want to do is call your new boss and tell them that you are having car troubles. Make sure that you have had the oil changed and that you have a full tank of gas. Make sure that the car is clean inside and out. If you can splurge, have it detailed. You will feel so in charge driving to work in your spiffed-up car.

If you take public transportation to work, make sure you have two weeks to a month's worth of tickets/passes/cards to get you into the office. You will be so busy learning your new job that you will not have time to do this later. Make sure you know the way to your new job. Take a dry run if you must, and make sure you do it during the time you normally commute. You will be shocked at how empty the roads can be if you drive in the middle of the day versus rush hour. Make sure you have an EZ pass if you need one, and make sure it is paid up. I didn't realize I needed that, and the $300+ in fines ruined my first month at my new job.

**Pets.** Don't forget your pets. If you have been home for an extended period, your pets have gotten used to that. Begin to get them used to the idea that you will not be there all day, especially if you will leave them on their own. Separation anxiety can be stressful for your pets. Get your dog used to being crated, if you did that, or just do some things outside the house to get your pet used to the idea of you no longer being home 24/7. Make sure to start adjusting their feeding times and bathroom breaks accordingly. Animals adapt very quickly to change, but not if it is abrupt. Make sure you pay your pets extra attention when you come home at night. They will have missed you, and they have believed in you as much, if not more, than your two-footed friends.

**Prepping Your Home and Team You, Inc. .** Make sure your house is cleaned and stocked. You will love coming home to a clean house the first night after you start a new job. You will not have the energy to clean it once you start work. Not at first.

Make some meals in advance. You might be too tired to make dinner the first few nights. You have no idea how exhausting returning to work is until you have done it. Have some nice dinners prepared and stored in the freezer if need be. Also, have plenty of things on hand to make lunch. Eating lunch out every day is expensive. If you must schedule any home repairs or inspections, do it before you go back to work. Don't forget services such as HVAC inspections or if you want to have the cable man/woman come out before going back to work. Schedule them now while you still can be at home.

If there is a movie you were dying to see, treat yourself to it. Take the family. If you want to see a museum exhibit, make sure you do so. It will be a while until you can take a day or two off.

**Most Importantly, Say Thank You.** One thing I did do to get ready to face the job world was to have more than one last hurrah. It provided a nice closure for me. I have a few friends who have gone back to school or were stay-at-home moms. One of the very few upsides I had while unemployed was being able to spend time with them. We went on walks and to museums (in D.C., almost all the museums are free). We had book clubs and coffees and generally just checked in with each other. I carefully calendared out days to spend with each one of my friends to transition back to work and thank them for their support. We hit places that had quickly become old haunts, updated each other on ongoing projects, celebrated my success, set up the next steps for each other on our continued journeys. I have already said this before, but it bears repeating: Nothing shows you who your friends are than something like losing your job. It is easy to be there for someone in the face of an immediate tragedy, but how your friends treat you afterward is the real definer. Some friends dropped me when I lost my job. Others just gradually drifted away. It was heartbreaking because, in those moments, every awful, horrible thing you believe about yourself is reflected in their actions.

However, there are the bright shining moments when the person you have a strong but sporadic friendship with sends you love and support out of the blue. When another sends you multiple four-figure checks because they have walked in the shoes in which you are currently traveling. When another friend hears the pain in your voice as you try to cover your depression and anxiety as you cancel an outing because you are just so ashamed and don't feel like you have the bandwidth to shower and go for a cup of coffee. An hour later, they are standing on your doorstep just to make sure you are OK.

Tragedy and adversity make us better. It is also how we discover who genuinely loves us and who merely tolerates us. It helps us to learn how we treat other people and how they should treat us. It is a miraculous initiation that helps us reconstruct and realign our lives to the things that are and should be important to us. My goal in going through any hardship is to come out of it a better person. If I don't do that, then all the adversity has been for nothing. I hope I came out of all this better, and that is also my hope for you, the Reader, the CEO of You, Inc. You will get through this, and although you have no or little control of the tragedy that hits your life, you have complete control on you handle it. My hope is that this little book has somehow helped you achieve that wish.

**Miscellaneous Preparation.** There is a plethora of things you should do before returning to work. Your first instinct might be to start your new job as soon as you can but make sure you give yourself enough time to tidy up loose ends so that you can focus on doing your best at the new job. With drug tests and having to start work on orientation days, you usually have at least one or two weeks to take care of things. Make sure you use that time wisely.

A few things to consider wrapping up before Day One of your new job:

- Are there any major family/friend birthdays or events coming up? Do you have to buy gifts or cards?
- Any doctor's appointments to schedule?
- Prep for the day ahead, not just the first day but every day. Lay out your keys, clothes, and anything else you need for work. This gives you time in the morning to spend quietly or with your family rather than rushing around looking for that new ID badge.

You will want to focus all your energy and available time on your new job. This is an incredibly stressful and exhausting process, almost as taxing to you as losing your job was. More importantly, you must put your best foot forward. Coming in late and needing to leave for doctor's appointments do not leave a good impression. If you must do these things in your first month or so at a new job, let your manager or recruiter know right away. Employers are very understanding that appointments have been made and that life happens. However, it is best to use these good graces only when you inescapably have to.

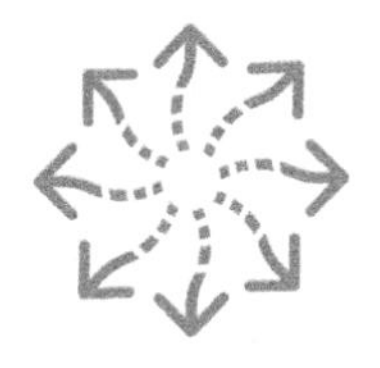

# 11

# GOING BACK TO WORK

Your return-to-work journey does not end once you receive a job offer. With any luck, as you read this you are about to start or have already resumed work. Congratulations. I do know the relief and satisfaction you feel. As I have already told you many times, you deserve this, and I want you to celebrate this fantastic accomplishment. I also want to give you a few words of warning based on the mistakes I have made. I want you to return to work purposefully and with a strategy. All along, I have asked you to think of this unemployed period as a time of self-discovery and planning. Not just day-to-day planning—I encourage you to be mindful and to make sure the daily routine you established carried over into your long-term vision for yourself. I also stressed self-care. I made many mistakes while unemployed, but the biggest mistake I made was that when I went back to work, I threw out my carefully written plan and my "wants" for myself and my career. I try not to be too hard on myself for this, and I would not be hard on you either. A paycheck, benefits, and the sheer joy of returning to work is nothing to sneeze at. So yes, take that job, get on your feet, but do not forget your vision. And your first step is to continue your extreme and mindful self-care.

One of the biggest mistakes you can make is to think that everything is back to normal now that you have gone back to work. Throughout life, you will hear the cliché that the only constant is change. It's true. Once you have gone through something as life-altering as losing your job, you cannot unring the bell. You have gone through an enormous change, and you need to move forward accordingly. Even if you were to assume your old job in the same organization with the same people, you have been through a change that they have not experienced. Remember, losing a job adds as much stress to a person as losing a spouse. For you to carry on as if nothing has changed would be imprudent at best. Everything you have gone through in losing your job and being unemployed has had an impact on you. That impact does not go away once you start a new role. You are not the same person you were weeks or months ago. You will be taking on a new way of life. Here are some steps to help you acclimate to what will be your new now and your future.

## Getting Past Trauma

Whether you have been unemployed for a day, a month, or a year, you have been through something life changing. Whether you have $20 or $200,000 in the bank, whether you have an independently wealthy partner or one who is dependent, you, my friend, have been through trauma. Trauma is a scary thing. The word itself conjures up visions of tragedy, mayhem, and destruction. Trauma is such a vast entity that we barely speak its name. It is not a word used lightly. Trauma is one of those things that people avoid discussing because of the discomfort level and the stigma attached to it.

What kind of a world do we live in that when something happens to us beyond our control, we feel shame about it? As if we are somehow responsible for the pain we have suffered. Worse, when you find the courage to speak of trauma, people avoid you and the topic. Why? There is a shame about being a victim—that perhaps you had something to do with the event, even though it probably was beyond your control. This is true of any trauma. I had a college friend who was violently attacked her freshman year. The attack was sexual, physical, and psychological at the same time. Yet, the victim was blamed. I will never understand how she was able to shoulder that burden at such a young age. Now that we are adults, she and I can talk about it, but as young college students, it rarely came up beyond a *How are you*? I thought I was respecting her privacy. I am sure she was going through her own issues, and we never discussed it. It was very recently, when we had both landed jobs after being unemployed, that she commented that during trauma, you more or less move through it. It is only in retrospect that you realize all that you have gone through.

Trauma is the response to a deeply distressing or disturbing event. After trauma a person may feel overwhelmed and unable to function day to day. Trauma can impact the ability to cope to "routine life", causes feelings of helplessness, diminishes their sense of self and their ability to feel the full range of emotions and experiences. It does not discriminate and it is pervasive throughout the world. Here is the thing about trauma: it is defined by the survivor. One person's anecdote is another person's crisis. As I said earlier, we often define ourselves by our work. To lose your identity is traumatic. The stress of reduced or no income, health issues brought on by said trauma, feelings of failure, and judgments of others only add to feelings of guilt, depression, anxiety, or worse. It is no wonder losing a job is traumatic.

We so often only regard the visual that we see on the surface. Going back to work can be like that. My father lost his job when I was a teenager, which was difficult for us as a family, but within nine months, he found another job, and we went right back to his normal; our normal. But the damage went unchecked and was the catalyst that ruined our family. We never recovered financially, but that wasn't the worst of it. My parents drifted apart. No one spoke with us kids about it, so we spent years walking on eggshells. My father's ego never recovered. And in the end, we just couldn't get past things. We were never a family unit again.

And you, my friend, have gone through the trauma of losing your job. It is ironic that you have no choice but to react as you are handling the trauma. You go through your day, manage your money, look for a new job, pray, spend time with your family, and then once you have a job, all too often you think the problem is solved. You have a job, you have an income and insurance, so you are fine. But you aren't. Trauma impacts us in a unique way. You can almost tuck the trauma away in a recess of your brain and psyche, hiding it as you go on through life. But I promise you; it finds a way to dig itself out and show its ugliness.

Our minds and bodies have in place fascinating mechanisms that allow us to survive the things that could hurt us and even to wage battle as we experience crisis. This is one of the astonishing ways we survive as a species and as individuals. Physiologically, our bodies go into overdrive while we experience trauma. When faced with an unexpected but devastating event, we go into survival mode. Adrenaline pumps through our systems and survival mechanisms kick in to protect us from the things that hurt us. We come up with a way to physically and emotionally keep going. Our body protects us in multiple ways, with that adrenaline kick to keep us going and sometimes even with the intense need for the rest and break that comes with sleep. Everyone reacts to trauma in different ways. Just as our bodies protect us, so do our minds. Sometimes, in particularly heinous cases, our minds protect us by taking our memories of a particularly horrible event. Sometimes we go numb, as if to shield ourselves from the intense barrage of emotions triggered by a traumatic event. Eventually, we go into survival mode. And sometimes survival mode becomes our normal.

As initially protective and shielding as our systems are, they cannot forever protect us from what has happened. Eventually, especially if the trauma is not addressed correctly, we experience Post Traumatic Stress Disorder, also known as PTSD. The symptoms of PTSD are as vast as their effects and unique to the individual sufferer. Victims of PTSD can have any variation of the symptoms to different degrees, but what all victims have in common is a triggering traumatic event. PTSD symptoms include:

- Constant anger/anxiety
- Mood swings
- Being easily startled
- High blood pressure
- Headaches
- Body aches for no reason
- Insomnia
- Depression
- Insomnia
- Erratic sleep patterns
- Oversleeping
- Lack of appetite
- Binge eating
- Uncharacteristic drinking of alcohol
- Recreational drug use

Each of these symptoms stresses the body. When we experience more than one of these symptoms, especially over a prolonged period, it can be debilitating. Often the symptoms are so innocuous that we overlook them while experiencing trauma and after it. Worse, if you are so used to trauma that this is your actual normal, the result can be lethal. We treat the symptom, not the cause. We take a sleep aid to combat depression. We attribute body aches to getting old. We take an analgesic to get past a headache. Do we ever stop to think that all these symptoms might not be the main issue but instead contributing signs of the bigger issues or trauma and PTSD? Rarely, if ever.

While I was out of work, I thought that going to therapy would be a great thing to help me cope with unemployment. A sad reality of our medical system was that try as I might, I could not find a therapist who took Medicaid. Once I was back in the work world, I was too busy for therapy and could not figure out how I would fit in appointments when I left for work at 5:30 a.m. to get to the office on time, and most nights was lucky if I got home before six. So few therapists offered weekend or evening hours. Then came COVID, when the world went virtual, and I no longer had a commute. Within a few weeks of sheltering in place, I found a therapist—the main driver being that I desperately needed a psychiatrist to renew my anxiety medication, which was a necessary evil thanks to the pandemic. Luckily, the practice I chose had therapists in their office. My first few sessions went well until my therapist asked me why I was coming to her. She said from her view; I seemed OK. I told her that was the problem. I refused to believe that I had gone through everything I had gone through over the past couple of years and come out OK. After another month of digging, she told me that she was finally what I was talking about. As she and I went into our roles of emotional excavators, we finally unearthed residual trauma. Things began to surface.

What my therapist saw in me she mistook for resilience. As humans, we are able to seemingly overcome trauma quickly. But resilience is not just the appearance of normalcy; it is the actual healing from the trauma. Given the right tools and environment, it is possible to heal. However, if we do not give ourselves that chance, if we bounce back without acknowledging what we have gone through and address that, we are caught in the awful cycle of the trauma never leaving us. That is PTSD.

An irony of the human body is that in the throes of trauma, physiologically, our body has one mission: to get us through this so that every part of us fires on all cylinders to keep us safe and get us to the other side. Two things can happen in this process: We come out of the trauma shortly, resilience kicks in. We overcome the trauma, or the trauma lingers and goes unaddressed, and our body eventually begins to feel the toll. We are not meant to be in flight-or-fight mode for long stretches of time. We appear to be resilient and healed on the surface because the surface issue of needing a job is addressed. However, what we are thinking and feeling underneath is the actual issue. All too often, we contribute those feelings to the stress of a new job or financial anxiety. Rarely do we think this is a carryover from being unemployed because that problem is resolved. But it is only resolved on the surface. Just like treating only the symptoms of PTSD, having a new job doesn't treat the underlying trauma. Having a job is just handling your symptoms of unemployment and financial worry. This is why we sleep, need breaks and rest, and take vacations. Our body needs to take that time to heal itself. When you go from unemployed to employed, you are taking yourself from one major event to another that requires you to be "on" at all times. This is why extreme self-care is mandatory. You must give your mind and body a chance to recover from one stressful event before going into another. If you followed extreme self-care from Day ONE of being unemployed, you are better equipped to handle the impact of trauma. I am not saying that everyone who suffers from unemployment is doomed to suffer PTSD. That is for you and hopefully a professional to decide. But I do have suggestions to help you continue to lead a mentally and physically healthy life as you assume your new role.

## Celebrate

Early on, when I suggested you put aside some money to do something to help you celebrate when you get a new job, it probably sounded a bit silly. But now that you have cause to celebrate, it probably seems like a good idea. It is a part of being human that we want to have closure as we close old chapters and start new ones. One of the reasons events such as losing a spouse or a job are so traumatic is that we seldom have time to prepare, and the transition period can be so abrupt. Celebrations are entirely different in that we know they are coming and can prepare for them and control them. We can take back ownership. Plus, if your life has been devoid of pleasure and joy, now you have a cause to revel.

Be mindful of your celebration. Plan it. If you have a family, plan a special meal to close the chapter of unemployment and look forward to a more stable future. Use your celebration as a means to thank those who stood by you. How you celebrate will be and should be special to you. When I knew I was going back to work, I scheduled several outings with friends, knowing that the new travel and responsibilities of my job would probably mean that we would not be able to get together anytime soon. I took three solid days and scheduled coffees and small meals in different cities to thank my friends who stood by me, talk about my accomplishment, and plan the future. It was a very cathartic experience. Although I like to think I appreciated my friends throughout the unemployment process, it felt good to acknowledge everyone for how they had stood by me. A few of my friends were unemployed at the same time I was. Months later, my friend Mary got a new job and told me that our small coffee had been so important to her because it gave her hope that she would find a job soon. (Within two months of my finding work, Mary did too.)

Additionally, several friends helped me out by lending me money. I took time during my celebratory visits to discuss repayment schedules and plans. But most of all, we spent time simply enjoying each other's company-- which is the foundation of friendship.

Take the opportunity of your celebration to talk out with others about what you have learned from the experience of being out of work and what you might do for success in your new role. Talk out your fears and concerns but also how this role will factor in your future success. I would also suggest scaling your celebration to your means. If you have been without an income for a year and have an urge to celebrate a new job by going away for a weekend, I would hold off on that. Save the big celebration for when you feel successful and comfortable in your new job. Think of this as closing the chapter and maybe rethink how and what you celebrate in the future.

## Money

This is a tough and dicey topic to talk about, but it's essential to discuss unemployment and your return to work. One of the largest temptations you will have once you find a new job may be to spend like you did when you were last employed, or at the very least to justify splurges.

This is especially true if you have a family. You have no doubt asked your partner and children to cut back, and it is tempting to reward them by replacing treats and perks that you trimmed from your family budget when you lost your job. Fight that feeling.

As parents, you and your partner are the decision-makers. However, that does not mean that you should not include the rest of the family. By being honest you help children understand the value of money and the need to save and make smart financial decisions. Think of it this way: Somehow, you have managed to navigate your family this far and things will look up once you have a job. Decide as a family how to make those smart financial decisions. You will be giving them an outstanding education. As you recover financially, consider tracking things for yourself and making it into a kind of game for your kids. Show them how much their scaling back is helping. Track how much you are saving. Show how you are paying off credit cards. Ask for their input. Have conversations about how to use money: *We can order pizza tonight or cook the pasta from ingredients in the pantry and put an extra $15 towards our savings.* This will help you and your children and partner make smart choices together.

You need to take a long look first at your obligations and then at your household budget. What bills have you held off that need to be paid right away? Most of this should be obvious —mortgage/rent, car payment, utilities, credit card bills. This can be particularly challenging because we feel as if we have failed when we cannot meet our basic financial needs, let alone when we cannot have the occasional indulgence. We need to learn to give ourselves a break. By bringing your children into the conversation, you show them that they are more important than money.

Finance is an area in life that sometimes eludes me. I have gone from periods of being comfortable and to periods of being rocky. Life is just easier for some people than for others. When the day is done you need to know that you have done the best you could. I used to get so depressed reading articles about how to prepare for the future. Sometimes I excelled at that; other times, I did not. Most experts give formulaic advice such as you need to have a 401K and have at least six months' expenses in savings. I wish. The reality is that most Americans are living paycheck to paycheck. A rare few have enough money for retirement. In my family, it was all over the map. My grandparents were frugal and lucky and retired early. My mother died penniless, and my father passed away massively in debt.

COVID has made us rethink our spending and how we plan. As I write this, we are emerging from a year of social distancing and staying in place in my state of Maryland. Countries such as Italy, China, and even some states are starting to look at returning to normal life, and the economy is the main driver. I do not wish ill will on anyone, but I feel oddly calm when I hear that major organizations such as The Cheesecake Factory and J.Crew are struggling to pay rent or filing for bankruptcy. If these giants could not prepare for being closed for even two months, what chance did I have to weather the storm for six months? I know it is not quite that simple, but it does give you the impression that few entities are following the experts. Or that they can afford to. So be easy on yourself.

I cannot emphasize that just like after a trauma, the goal is to get you whole again. Just as everyone's time of unemployment is different, so is your recovery. I had two main financial priorities in the first few months of having a new job: to catch up on bills and to be sure I could meet the expenses of going to my new job.

And that is a tough one that people don't often consider. You forget that in some ways, having a job costs money—money you were not spending while unemployed. My new job required a minimum commute of two hours a day, plus tolls. I found out about the tolls the hard way. There was gas and maintenance on my car. Then there are things like lunches and new clothes needed for a new job. My new employer was generous enough to give employees insurance on Day One, which meant that I could see a doctor. That also meant I had copays and coinsurance. I initially breathed a sigh of relief that I now had a matching 401K. Then I realized I couldn't afford to contribute to it. It can all add up very quickly. Make sure you can meet your new budget before making major changes in your spending and before you try to go back to what once was.

Choose your financial moves wisely. I set my priority on catching up on things. Your priorities will look different from mine. The important thing is that you do things thoughtfully and strategically. Chances are that you had no or very little control over losing your job. So now that you have the opportunity to be strategic, be strategic. As I took my new role, I had a personal_obligation in Santa Fe, New Mexico, my first week of employment. Because I took this commitment, serving on the alumni board of my alma mater, I went on the trip believing I had just enough money to go. I was staying with a friend and the airfare was already paid for. But life is always more expensive than we think it will be. I had not factored in incidentals. Plus, a friend who lives in Santa Fe and I always managed to sneak in a little time at a local spa. I was not missing out on that. In retrospect, the trip and spa visit were a foolish indulgence. I could have attended the meeting via teleconference, and as much as I enjoyed the time with my friend, the $150+

I spent at the spa could have gone to more important things. I made some errors in judgment that pushed back my recovery.

A year into my new job, I have managed to get all my bills caught up, begun to pay back friends, and to stock up on goods during COVID. All of this came with a lot of sacrifices. But they were worth it. I have raised my credit score more than eighty points (yes, it had gotten that low) and managed to pay more than thirty percent of my debt—a huge accomplishment. All my bills are up to date, and I even have a modest emergency fund—not six months' worth, but enough. Had I tried to pick up where my old life left off, I would not have been able to catch up so much.

## Therapy

I mentioned that I decided to go to therapy after returning to work. In therapy I did not feel the need to talk about my parents' mistakes or any deep-seated issues. For me, going to therapy was just part of what you get out of an annual physical. You rarely go to a physical thinking that there is something wrong with you. Most of the time, we go because a partner has nagged us, because we get a discount on our insurance deductible, or because we are curious to see what is happening under the hood. And for the most part, we get a thumbs-up from the doctor and maybe a little lecture on something we always knew, such as the need to lose a few pounds or to cut back on saturated fats. And we all know the story of the outliers—those people who found out something in a physical that saved their lives in the long run. I looked at therapy that way. I found it hard to believe that I had escaped the past year or so without having some issues after losing a loved one to cancer, being in a hostile work situation, losing my job for a year, and then undergoing the stress of starting a new one. I thought and still do, that the healthiest thing would be to see a therapist just to find out what was going on and to get an objective opinion about whether I truly needed to work on myself further. From my perspective, it would either give me peace of mind or help me straighten out a few things. Who knows, maybe mentally I was in that tiny percentage that had something life-threatening out there that we would catch in time. Consider this for yourself. You may not think therapy is your thing, but how do you know unless you have tried it with a good therapist?

## Continue Extreme Self Care

Why is it we never take care of ourselves the way we should? In this book, I have encouraged you to treat yourself well by taking care of yourself—exercising, meditating, journaling, reading, spending time with friends and family. Self-care for each of us is very different. I had a fantastic routine in place when I received my job. My routine made me so happy that I couldn't wait to get up each morning to begin. It took me months to craft it into what I considered a rich and rewarding daily experience. It made me happy, and truthfully, it was the first time in almost two years I felt good about myself and the future. What took months to craft and hone took mere days to destroy.

As I took on my new job and my days became filled, one by one, habits and practices that had taken me weeks to perfect and solidify crumbled under the pressure of a two-hour commute, needing to learn a new role, fitting in housekeeping, and the demands of being human. When I dropped the first habit of daily meditation, convinced I could do it once I got into the office and then convinced I would do it when I got home, it became too much. I was sure that I could fit in daily journaling at lunch, but like most Americans, I spent lunchtime at my desk working. Gatherings with friends soon flew to the wayside and the weekends. I was convinced that I could do my daily reading time via Audible in the car ride back and forth to work, but the drain on my cell battery was too much, and by the time I got home, I was done. Thus, all of that oh-so-careful extreme self-care went out the window.

Part of it was that I thought I could do in a few hours what I had previously spent a whole day doing—another one of my mistakes not to repeat. Understand that we spend more time at work than anywhere else, even sleeping. So this is, of course, the biggest demand of our day. You must carve out time for yourself as you adjust to a new job, especially quiet moments of reflection. If you were one of those types like me and you scheduled and tracked your daily activities, I recommend taking a few moments to think about what you value and what you want to keep. What is your priority? I do not include family time with that. That is another matter you should discuss with your family and with your partner. Give each of yourselves even 30 minutes of free self-care time each day. You will be happier, and thus, your family will be happier. As you become adjusted to your new work routine, you may find other opportunities to add to your self-care. I am currently learning Swedish on the commute home. In getting back to your new normal, don't forget the practices that have served you well in survival mode.

It is understandable to think that once you have a job, most if not all of your worries are over. Sadly, the opposite is true. It is very easy to fool yourself that your time of stress is over simply because you are dealing with a new kind of stress. When you are out of work, you are worried about money, paying bills, medical issues. Those lessons disappear when you have a job because suddenly you have money in your bank account, and you know that more money will be coming in. You suddenly have insurance and a place to go. You are trading one type of stress for another. As we discussed, stress is one of the single worst things that can happen to the body, triggering a physiological and emotional response. It can bring with it fear and anxiety as well. Instead of wondering if we will ever get a job, often, we convert that fear into the negative thought pattern of "Will I keep this job?" Not only that but there is also FOMO—Fear of Missing Out—when taking a new job. People become convinced that they made the wrong choice. They are victimized by the trauma they have experienced, first by losing work and then by being out of work. The negative thought process takes hold, and it is one of the hardest cycles to shake. In addition to that, sometimes, when someone has landed better than they had hoped, they experience guilt (for those left behind) and imposter syndrome. All of this puts a huge amount of stress on the body. Therefore, it is essential to create and cultivate a comfortable, quiet, and safe place for yourself. Extreme self-care is one way to do that and to counteract the effects of stress and anxiety.

## Staying Open to Opportunity

I hope you landed your dream job. Or at the very least landed somewhere that makes you very happy for a very long time. But, if you took a job to be practical—and I don't care what that recruiter told me, there is nothing wrong with that—it is perfectly acceptable to continue looking. Put your best efforts into the job you received. But if you know in your heart that this isn't where you belong, keep looking. I have accepted jobs and continued to interview for other positions, but I still gave my all during the hours I worked. You need to do that, too. Think of it as investing but not attaching. As I often say in this book, I want you to think about work differently. I want your priority to be You, Inc. That might mean taking what you can get now and looking for something better. That does not mean making a poor effort while at the organization that believed in you and is giving you a paycheck and benefits. They deserve your hard work and your loyalty. They do not deserve the rest of your life and your obsequiousness. While you were unemployed, if you decided to go back to school to get a computer certification or learn about journalism and you found a job that lets you do those things, take the job. While you are there, work hard. Ultimately, keep your mission and vision in mind. I do not want you to give up what you want for yourself. Think of this job as a stopping point in your career where you can learn and, more importantly, where you can contribute.

Continue to develop a strategic routine of reflecting so you can plan your next career steps. Be open to other opportunities, both within and outside of your organization. Most organizations love to hire from within. And why shouldn't they? It costs three to ten times a person's salary to replace them when they leave. According to a 2018 article by Gartner organization, over 40 percent of the employees surveyed said that lack of opportunity was the reason they left their jobs. If you break the group down further by generation, this feeling is shared by the current working Millennial and Generation Z employees, who will be almost seventy percent of our workforce in 2025. Employers are taking notice. By promoting individuals from within, organizations retain top talent who already know and understand their business and understand and fit in with their culture—traits that are highly valued. It is in your interest and your employers' interest to keep looking for opportunities within the organization.

After you have accepted a role, there is no harm in setting your LinkedIn profile to show that you are actively open to opportunities.

You can set your profile with a safeguard that does not let your current employer know, as long as you have properly updated your profile with your new employer's name. LinkedIn did this for a reason—they saw the trend. According to Forbes, more than 40 percent of employees surveyed indicated they were passively open to opportunities inside and outside their organization. An additional 25 percent said they are actively seeking something better. Plainly put, this means we are looking to improve and advance. I want you to do so wisely and intentionally. Who knows, you could receive an inquiry for your dream job or dream organization. At the very least you could learn that you have settled in the right place after all. Be open to opportunities as they come to you but also seek them out on your own. Do not wait for the promotion or dream job to come to you.

# SOME FINAL THOUGHTS

I set out to write this book to help people, including myself. I realized that I would be unable to do either unless I was transparent and willing to do what Patrick Lencioni calls being vulnerable. A couple of hard years that included losing a job and what I thought was the opportunity of a lifetime—the thing that would catapult me to where I wanted to be (finally!)— a year without an income, decimating my savings and 401K, crashing a pretty good credit score and losing a few people I had considered lifelong ride-or-die friends needed to end with sending myself to therapy. You might not feel something to that extent, but I felt I owed it to myself to go. On my first visit, the therapist asked me a wonderful question that I will now ask you: *What have you taken from all of this?*

One of our greatest gifts is the ability to reflect and learn from experience. In the views of adult learning, there are three common principles: We learn from *education*, such as reading, watching videos, lectures, etc.; *exposure*, such as being coached, corrected, and developed; and more than anything else, we learn from *experience,* by doing things. But without reflection and reinforcement, experience flounders and we forget. A way to retain a negative experience while protecting our psyche is to shift something from a negative to a positive. I did the former. I told you my intent in my writing this book was to have you learn from my mistakes. I got my job and was so happy I could start paying my bills and feel valued again that I took all the good habits I had created and stuffed them away into the culture of busy. I am encouraging you to do what it took me a further year to learn. My experience, as painful as it was, was also an amazing gift of opportunity. I learned just how tough I was. I learned exactly who my friends were. I learned that I could survive horrible things and still bounce back. But most importantly, I learned that what I truly had to offer was to help others. I want to help you learn from this experience.

## Friends

One of the most astounding things that will happen to you when you lose your job is that you will be amazed at who reaches out to you to provide support and who doesn't. When I left my job, I was more than a little hurt that the two employees I had hired never followed up with me. One I had hired them not because they could do the job but because they had genuine talent and I knew this job would transform their lives. They would have advantages that, as the eldest in a large family, they would never get otherwise. The other was someone who would benefit from the environment and have the chance to grow in the field or choose from multiple fields. Not a word from either. I attributed it to them being young and green. Maybe someone told them not to contact me. I was also surprised that employees with whom I had had very little interaction reached out to me in multiple ways. One sent flowers. Another sent me a bunch of gift cards. Many offered to be my reference. I was floored when a person who seemed to be one of my biggest nemeses in the workplace reached out to me. Not only that, but multiple people told me that upon hearing I was let go, this person had gone into my former boss's office and had read them the riot act so loudly that people could hear it down the hall. I was especially amused by this as I was told this person had repeatedly complained about me and that this was one of the reasons the company did not continue my employment. You never know where your next rave review may come from.

Without a doubt, one of the best things I learned from this experience was discovering who my friends were. Once I retained employment, multiple people reached out to me and asked for assistance gaining entry to my current company or prior ones. My answer with all of these people has been No. It is not revenge. But honestly, I have seen their true character and cannot in good conscience recommend them.

## Gratitude

One exercise I did every night was to write down three things for which I was grateful. I challenged myself to avoid writing the same things every night. In the words of Oprah, who talked about a similar exercise, there was a lot of food in there. Also, a lot of friends. I tried to be as specific as possible. What deed did my friend do that made me grateful? Sometimes I was lucky, and I could write down a job interview or phone call. I was determined to restart the process again. At the same time, I was social distancing, so I took the jar where I had carefully folded all my pieces of paper and made myself read all the things I was grateful for during that horrible, horrible period. I was shocked at how many things I had managed to find during such a painful time. So why is it that we find it so difficult to be grateful in good times?

I took all the piles of paper and gathered them into a metal pan and lit them on fire. By burning the papers on which I had carefully written my gratitude, I was following a ritual that you are making room for new things to enter your life by eliminating something. The jar now sits on my bedside table, and every night before turning in, I write down three things for which I am grateful. I force myself not to repeat and be open and honest. By the end of the year, I will reread my thoughts. Above all, I hope I do not lose this practice.

I honestly do not know many people who could have gotten through those two years and remained intact. And maybe I didn't, either. The point is that those two years ended. Finally, I got through the unemployment, lack of money, and all that came with it. I had found a way to survive. It was not easy. But I did it. No one will ever be able to take that away from me. In losing my job, I had lost a bit of my identity and also a tremendous amount of confidence of which I had a very small supply. I have always lacked confidence in myself, but one thing I had complete faith in was my ability to gain employment. I had never had an issue before. I would wake every day wondering why I was suddenly out of work — I, who always had multiple job offers and always received a counteroffer when I gave notice. One of my biggest fears in life was not having a job and not having an income. And there I was, living that nightmare and all its trappings for a year. The biggest gift is knowing that I have indeed come out of it. And you will too.

At the start of this book, I mentioned the parable of the man being stuck inside the hole, all alone. Finally, someone jumps into the hole with him. He is alone no more. You are now in that hole. You may think the sides are too steep for you to climb out. You may think it is too deep for you to jump out. You may think it is too dark for you to see. And worse, you may think you are alone. You are not. I have been in this once and similarly felt like I would never get out. But I did. I cannot get you out of this hole. I can only help make your time in the hole less upsetting and distressing, and I can point you to some of the tools to get yourself out of the hole. And you will get yourself out. And all I ask in return is that if you are walking down the street and hear someone else calling that they have fallen down the hole, you help them get out as I hope I have helped you.

# ABOUT THE AUTHOR

Sabina Sulat is an accomplished HR/Organizational Development and Learning executive. She has spent the better part of the past two decades studying how organizations function and how people work. She has been privileged to have learned and contributed to the work of multiple global and Fortune 1000/500 organizations and their employees, considering the primary goal of her works being to help others develop and improve.

In 2020, Sabina recognized the impact COVID-19 would have on the American worker, forcing millions of people to lose their jobs in the wake of the pandemic. Inspired by her own prior experience of having been out of work, she began working on a book to help others navigate the path of being unemployed. Her mission is to have people think of their period of unemployment as an opportunity to grow and learn. In the process of writing *Agile Unemployment,* Sabina realized that there was a major need to give people the steps required to "learn to be unemployed" and that she could help coach and support others to rethink their time of unemployment as the opportunity to build confidence and resilience. As a result, her organization **Re: Working** was born.

Through **Re: Working,** Sabina has taken what she has observed and accomplished and now dedicates herself and her business to helping others rethink and rework being unemployed as an opportunity rather than as a catastrophe. Her goal is to help people come out of the adversity of being unemployed more resilient and confident, prepared for the next phase of their career journey.

# ABOUT THE AUTHOR

# APPENDIX

# SCHEDULING YOUR PRIORITIES

As a coach, I am often asked what the exact schedule, order of tasks, and activities someone should follow to have a successful and productive unemployment period. Every person's experience will be different and will be influenced by their life and circumstances. What follows is a suggested order of events. Keep in mind that some of this might be influenced by the date of the month you are let go or by your family needs. It is best to get time-sensitive activities out of the way, such as applying for unemployment compensation and taking care of your medical issues. A suggested schedule is as follows:

## Day One

Get all essential paperwork, names, and information from HR, especially insurance and paycheck information.

- Clear any personal items from your desk/locker, if applicable and possible.
- Discuss the situation with someone—family, friend, or both.
- Do something nice for yourself—dinner, massage, etc.

## Day Two

File for unemployment compensation.

- File for Food Assistance/SNAP benefits.
- Review your/family medical needs, schedule appointments. Your work insurance, FSA, and HAS benefits expire at the end of the month.
- Begin to explore insurance exchanges.
- Begin to strategize!

## Week One

Begin to get your finances in order.

- Look at all your assets.
- Review monthly expenses.
- Identify areas to cut back.
- Make an appointment with a professional resume writer.
- Discuss your new job situation with close friends and family.

## Week Two

Begin to reflect on job choices, explore other roads if you wish.

- Write your mission and vision statements.
- Review network, begin building network areas if necessary.
- Assemble your Interview Kit. Check it weekly.
- Begin to build Home Kit, Car Kit, etc.

## Weeks Three and Four

Complete any items from Weeks One and Two that are still outstanding.

- Begin applying to new jobs using your new resume,
- Begin to structure your new Meaningful Extreme Self-Care and Development routine.

## Beginning of Month Two

By the start of Month Two (provided you did not lose your job at the end of the month), you should be in maintenance mode with most of the tasks and activities I have outlined in the book. You should be focusing on applying for work and your self-care routine. I suggest you take a hard look at all of your activities at the beginning of each month. See if you need to alter your approach or adjust your routine. Assess what is working and what is not. Keep the tasks and activities that bring you a sense of accomplishment or that you feel bring you closer to your goals and discard the activities that do not move you forward. Look at your finances and medical items to see if anything needs to be altered.

## Re-evaluate and Refresh

Job search methods

- Finances and budget
- Medical insurance and medical needs
- Change out your Interview Kit, if necessary
- Meaningful Extreme Self-Care/Development Plan

Although there is no guaranteed length of time you will be unemployed, you will continue to repeat Month Two, altering your plans according to your needs. If things feel stagnant, do not hesitate to change them as you are able.

# RESOURCES

The following were used for research and inspiration for this book.


"Authentic Happiness." *University of Pennsylvania*, www.authentichappiness.sas.upenn.edu/.

Bresciani, Alessio. "51 Mission Statements from The World's Best Companies." *Alessio Bresciani*, 10 Oct. 2020, www.alessiobresciani.com/foresight-strategy/51-mission-statement-examples-from-the-worlds-best-companies/.

Carroll, Ryder. *The Bullet Journal Method: Track the Past, Order the Present, Design the Future*. Portfolio, 2018.

"Changes in Stress after Meditation." *ScienceDaily*, US Army Research Laboratory, 21 June 2018, www.sciencedaily.com/releases/2018/06/180621111955.htm.

"Continuation of Health Coverage (COBRA)." *United States Department of Labor*, www.dol.gov/general/topic/health-plans/cobra.

Dattner, Ben. "The Psychology of Networking." *Psychology Today*, Sussex Publishers, 4 May 2008, www.psychologytoday.com/us/blog/credit-and-blame-work/200805/the-psychology-networking.

Forshee, Dr. Danielle. "Psychological Benefits of Routines." *Danielle Forshee, Psy.D, LCSW*, Dr. Danielle Foreshee, 2 July 2019, drdanielleforshee.com/psychological-benefits-of-routines/.

Frankl, Viktor E., et al. *Man's Search for Meaning: the Classic Tribute to Hope from the Holocaust*. Rider, an Imprint of Ebury Publishing, 2020.

HEALTHSTATUS TEAM. "Top 5 Stressful Situations." *HealthStatus*, 18 May

2017, www.healthstatus.com/health_blog/depression-stress-anxiety/top-5-stressful-situations/.

Hobson, Nick. "How Rituals Alter the Brain to Help Us Perform Better." *Psychology Today*, Sussex Publishers, Jan. 2017, www.psychologytoday.com/us/blog/ritual-and-the-brain/201709/how-rituals-alter-the-brain-help-us-perform-better#:~:text=There's%20now%20mounting%20scientific%20evidence,deeply%2C%20and%20solve%20more%20quickly.blog/ritual-and-the-brain/201709/how-rituals-alter-the-brain-help-us-perform-better#:~:text=There's%20now%20mounting%20scientific%20evidence,deeply%2C%20and%20solve%20more%20quickly.

"Join Me in Ending Hunger." *Donate to Feeding America - Feeding America*, secure.feedingamerica.org/site/Donation2?df_id=29690&29690.donation=form1&gclid=9eaad6d905e6172e33f8b60cdf9e20ca&gclsrc=3p.ds&&s_src=Y21XP4B1Y&s_subsrc=c&s_keyword=feeding+america+com&msclkid=9eaad6d905e6172e33f8b60cdf9e20ca.

Koretz, Joanna. "What Happens When Your Career Becomes Your Whole Identity." *Harvard Business Review*, 26 Dec. 2019, hbr.org/2019/12/what-happens-when-your-career-becomes-your-whole-identity.

Mager, Dan. "What You Need to Know About Stress and Self-Care." *Psychology Today*, Sussex Publishers, 29 Aug. 2017, www.psychologytoday.com/us/blog/some-assembly-required/201708/what-you-need-know-about-stress-and-self-care.

Marck-Sherk, Madeline. "The Importance of Routines for Athletes: Naples Sports Performance Training - Naples Sports Performance Training: Gulf Coast Performance." *Naples Sports Performance Training | Gulf Coast Performance*, Naples Sports Performance Training | Gulf Coast Performance, 30 Dec. 2020, www.gulfcoastperform.com/blog/the-importance-of-routines-for-athletes.

Miller, Caroline Adams, et al. *Creating Your Best Life: the Ultimate Life List Guide*. Sterling Publishing Co., 2020.

Mortimer, Jeylan, et al. "How Unemployment Affects Twentysomethings'

Self-Worth." *Harvard Business Review*, 22 Dec. 2016, hbr.org/2016/12/how-unemployment-affects-twentysomethings-self-worth.

Navarro-Abal, Yolanda, et al. "Psychological Coping with Job Loss. Empirical Study to Contribute to the Development of Unemployed People." *International Journal of Environmental Research and Public Health*, MDPI, 20 Aug. 2018, www.ncbi.nlm.nih.gov/pmc/articles/PMC6122016/.

Onderko, Karen. "What Is Trauma?" *Integrated Listening*, Integrated Listening, 25 Oct. 2018, integratedlistening.com/blog/2018/09/13/what-is-trauma/.

Rao, Aliya Hamid. "When Losing Your Job Feels Like Losing Your Self." *Harvard Business Review*, 1 Feb. 2021, hbr.org/2020/04/when-losing-your-job-feels-like-losing-your-self.

Sandberg, Erica. "How to Pay Your Credit Card Bills in a Financial Emergency." *Experian*, Experian, 16 Mar. 2021, www.experian.com/blogs/ask-experian/how-to-pay-your-credit-card-bills-in-a-financial-emergency/?ty=mc&pc=crm_exp_0&cc=emm_f_m_act_9990920200421_mktfttFreeCCFinancialHardship_20200421_x-_101&cid=5844A3011F0BCDBC3B24AEF6E9B3D8440509377AB-B9C37D1CD68922DE39AA6B6.

Scott, Kris. *Where to Apply for Food Assistance in Every State*, 16 Aug. 2020, www.msn.com/en-us/money/personalfinance/where-to-apply-for-food-assistance-in-every-state/ss-BB13MRlV?li=BBnb7Kz#image=1.

Sinek, Simon. *Start with Why: How Great Leaders Inspire Everyone to Take Action*. Portfolio Penguin, 2019.

Snyder, C. R. "The Psychology of Hope." *Google Books*, Google, books.google.com/books?hl=en&lr=&id=b3bz8tzBvC0C&oi=fnd&pg=PR9&dq=-psychology%2Bof%2Bhope.&ots=PaXOC4_cow&sig=NwEYNHN-qHG3oEUy_5ke7db6LbzI#v=onepage&q=psychology%20of%20hope.&f=false.

"Supplemental Nutrition Assistance Program (SNAP)." *USDA*, 23 Apr. 2021, www.fns.usda.gov/snap/supplemental-nutrition-assistance-program.

Team, HealthStatus. "Top 5 Stressful Situations." *HealthStatus*, 18 May 2017, www.healthstatus.com/health_blog/depression-stress-anxiety/top-5-stressful-situations/.

Turczynski, Bart. "2021 HR Statistics: Job Search, Hiring, Recruiting & Interviews." *Zety*, 14 Apr. 2021, zety.com/blog/hr-statistics.

"We Are What We Do." *Meetup*, www.meetup.com/.

"When Losing Your Job Feels Like Losing Your Self." *Harvard Business Review*, 1 Feb. 2021, hbr.org/2020/04/when-losing-your-job-feels-like-losing-your-self.

White, Martha C. "Here's How Long It Really Takes to Get a Job." *Money*, 22 Oct. 2015, money.com/how-long-it-takes-to-get-hired/.

Zetlin, Minda. "The 9 Worst Mission Statements of All Time." *Inc.com*, Inc., 15 Nov. 2013, www.inc.com/minda-zetlin/9-worst-mission-statements-all-time.html.

Made in the USA
Las Vegas, NV
05 May 2024

89563212R00154